ODÙ IFÁ

THE ETHICAL TEACHINGS

Also by the Author

Kwanzaa: A Celebration of Family, Community and Culture

The African American Holiday of Kwanzaa:
A Celebration of Family, Community and Culture

The Book of Coming Forth By Day:
The Ethics of the Declarations of Innocence

Essays on Struggle: Position and Analysis

Introduction to Black Studies

Kawaida: A Communitarian African Philosophy

Kawaida Theory: An Introductory Outline

Kemet and the African Worldview (co-editor)

Kwanzaa: Origins, Concepts and Practice

The Million Man March / Day of Absence:
A Commemorative Anthology (co-editor)

The Million Man March / Day of Absence Mission Statement

Reconstructing Kemetic Culture

Selections from the Husia: Sacred Wisdom of Ancient Egypt

ODÙ IFÁ

THE ETHICAL TEACHINGS

TRANSLATION AND COMMENTARY
A KAWAIDA INTERPRETATION

MAULANA KARENGA

Preface by Wande Abimbola, Àwíṣẹ Àgbáyé

UNIVERSITY OF SANKORE PRESS
LOS ANGELES
1999

Odù Ifá: The Ethical Teachings
Translation and Commentary, A Kawaida Interpretation

ISBN 0-943412-22-6

For information write to the University of Sankore Press below.

University of Sankore Press
3018 West 48th Street
Los Angeles, CA 90043
(800) 997- 2656

For our people everywhere.

Fún àwọn èǹìyàn wa níbi-gbogbo.

Kwa watu wetu kila mahali.

PREFACE

It gives me a great pleasure to write a few words about this new and exciting work of Dr. Maulana Karenga which I have read with considerable interest. This monumental work is undoubtedly an excellent scholarly addition to the rich and growing body of translations, commentaries, expositions and interpretations of the *Odu Ifa*, a task which started at the turn of this century with the works of D. Onadele Epega, E.M. Lijadu and A.F. Beyioku. Professor Karenga's current work on the ethical teachings of Ifa will certainly set the tone for similar studies of Ifa as we enter another millennium. His contributions in this volume are to my mind important in the following respects.

First, he has carefully researched existing published texts of Ifa which are available in Yoruba with accompanying English and French translations and pulled out from them a wide range of ethical and moral teachings. Some of these were not immediately accessible because the texts are out-of-print and therefore no longer in circulation. Thus, he provides for us a large volume of texts on Ifa ethical teachings which are of immense value beyond the world of scholarship. Indeed, this book will be useful to the general reader as well as those who are interested in enriching themselves with the philosophy and moral teachings of ancient and modern Africa.

Much more important are the interpretations of the texts contained in this volume which Professor Karenga has developed with tremendous insight. He has brought to bear in this volume his rich background in the translation and interpretation of ancient Egyptian texts which is characterized by a commendable combination of scholarship and sensitivity to the texts. I find his interpretation of Ifa texts contained in this volume to be very profound and thought-provoking. Furthermore, Professor Karenga has been very careful in the way he has handled the texts, thus, preserving their original poetic and philosophical import even in the English translation. Only a scholar and a teacher who is deeply connected with and highly committed to the preservation and dissemination of African culture and values can see the need to treat the texts with such profound respect.

This volume should put to rest the speculations of writers who have ignorantly stated that African religions and societies are not concerned with moral values. This present work of Dr. Karenga demonstrates how greatly committed African societies have always been to imparting and disseminating cogent and essential moral values from one generation to another. I deeply appreciate this volume of the ethical teachings of Ifa and highly recommend it as a useful, informative, and excellent work.

Wande Abimbola, Àwíṣẹ Àgbáyé
Professor of African Religions and Cultures,
Boston University

Introduction

Overview of the Project

The *Odù Ifá*, the sacred text of the spiritual and ethical tradition of Ifa, is one of the great sacred texts in the world and a classic of African and world literature. Its sacred narratives and divination focus have been well-discussed, but less attention has been given to the rich resource it offers in ethical teachings. This book seeks to address this inadequacy of attention. Its governing interest is to present the ethical teachings of the *Odù* in the language of modern moral discourse while at the same time preserving and building on its distinctiveness as an ancient body of moral literature capable of framing and inspiring modern ethical philosophical reflection.

Furthermore, this book represents a larger effort to provide a modern translation of an ancient text with accompanying commentary which serve as both an *interpretation* and *transmission* of this classical African ethical tradition, the *Ifá* tradition of the Yoruba. This project is conducted within the Kawaida tradition which defines itself as an ongoing synthesis of the best of African thought and practice in constant exchange with the world. Moreover, *Kawaida* philosophy maintains that we must constantly dialog with African culture in the ongoing quest to become and be the best of what it means to be African and human in the fullest sense. This requires that we constantly ask questions and seek answers from African culture to the fundamental and enduring concerns of human life--concerns of transcendence and everyday life, of human meaning and the human prospect, of the good life, the moral person, the just society and the good world. This engagement of the Odu is carried out within this philosophical understanding.

In addition, the project is one in which tradition is approached not simply as a process or context into which one comes, but also as an ongoing product of one's effort to understand and engage it. Thus, within the framework of this engagement, a Kawaida approach evolves which represents not only reaffirmation and continuity, but also change in focus and ongoing development of the particular tradition of Ifa as well as African culture in general. In this, we observe the Kawaida principle that everything we do must be based on *tradition* and *reason*. Tradition is our foundation, our cultural grounding, and reason, especially moral reasoning, is a mode of engagement that aids us in our ongoing efforts to understand and practice tradition in new and expanded ways and to keep it as a living, vibrant and rich source of the best of human thought and practice.

In this thrust we have in a real sense begun to build a Kawaida or African American form of Ifa tradition in the same sense that forms of the way of Ifa have evolved in Brazil as Candomblé, Cuba as Lukumí, Haiti as Voudun, and Puerto Rico as Lukumí. Again, then, we approach our tradition--continental as well as diasporan tradition--not simply as a context or process in which we come, but also as an ongoing product of our efforts to understand and engage it and constantly enrich and expand it as a living, valuable and instructive way of being human in the world.

The Odu Ifa is a corpus of sacred texts designed essentially to answer questions of human life through the process of divination. But as Awiṣẹ Wande Abimbola has pointed out in his seminal works on the Odu, they contain a wealth of knowledge and teachings in the realm of various fields including art, literature, medicine, history, religion and ethics.

The fundamental thrust of the Kawaida interpretation of the Odu Ifa is to shift the almost exclusive focus on divination by adherents and scholars to an essentially ethical focus. To do this one must first search for and extract explicit and implicit moral teaching and critically discuss them, giving due attention to the delicate task of balancing assumptions concerning ancient meanings with modern moral interpretations and concerns. Secondly, given the centrality of the concept and practice of sacrifice (*ìrúbọ*) in the Ifa tradition, an expanded understanding of *ìrúbọ* must be established. *Kawaida* understands sacrifice in two basic ways--as *ritual performance* and as *moral practice*. In ritual performance, the thing offered is an object; in moral practice, what is offered is oneself. Thus, ritual sacrifice is *object-giving* and moral sacrifice is *self-giving*.

At this point it is important to note two things. First, sacrifice as object-giving does not mean that one does not self-give at one level, but clearly the main and overriding focus is on the giving of objects. Likewise, sacrifice as self-giving does not mean one does not give objects, i.e., valuables, but clearly the principal and determining focus is on the giving of self. Secondly, a critical and expanded reading of the text offers an opportunity for both object-giving and self-giving exclusively or collectively. For example, the Odu Ogbedi (21:1) says:

> *Ogbedi Perepere was the one who*
> *interpreted the teachings of Ifa for Ori*
> *Who had kneeled down and chosen his destiny,*
> *And whom detractors were preventing from*
> *achieving it.*
> *Ifa says he sees the evil-wishers who do not want us*
> *to succeed in what we are doing.*
> *Ifa says he will join us in overcoming the*
> *evil-wishers.*

He says we should sacrifice.
When Ori had done all that was due in
practicing sacrifice,
All that he was doing fell into place and
straightened out.
And the way became clear.

Now, when Ifa says "he will join us in overcoming the evil-wishers." I read that as a call to cooperative struggle of the divinity and human person to achieve a good end. Furthermore, when Ifa says "we should sacrifice," I read that as a counsel to give more of self in the struggle, i.e., more dedication, more discipline, more effort. And when the text says that "After Ori had done all that was due in practicing sacrifice," all that he was doing fell into place and straightened 9out and the way became clear." I take sacrifice to mean an expanded dedication, discipline and effort--in a word, an *expanded giving of self* through which he prospered and his way became clear.

Indeed, as Kawaida teaches, the *clear way* and the *good life* require a *morality of sacrifice*. And the teachings of *Odu Ifa* offer an excellent source for framing and grounding such a morality. In a contemporary context of commercially cultivated self-indulgence and therapeutic consumerism, a morality of sacrifice becomes a central pillar in the ongoing thrust to envision and pursue possibilities of human freedom and flourishing in society, history and our daily lives.

Finally, in this regard, the Odu teach that ritual sacrifice without moral character and practice is of no value. In the Odu Irete'yeku (70:1), it says:

Orifusi, father of Elu, was searching for a way
to avoid death,
So that death would not kill him, his children
or his wives.
They said: if you want to avoid death,
You must sacrifice and follow the teachings of Ifa.
Ifa will teach you the conduct and character
Which will enable you to avoid death.
They said: if you sacrifice, you should begin
doing good more than ever before.
For your sacrifice is useless, if your character
is deficient.

The text goes on to advise Orifusi to take the chickens and pigeons he had for sacrifice home and release them. Also, he was told to not kill them but to give them food. And finally, the divine ones say to him, "And you must not kill anything whatsoever from this day on. For one who does not want death to kill him, should not kill anything whatsoever either."

The text clearly tells us that sacrifice as ritual performance is not sufficient in itself. In fact, it calls one's ritual performance useless, invalid, or in vain (*lásan*) if one's character is deficient (*dín*). Moreover, the text says, Ifa will teach us "the conduct and character" necessary to achieve our end. And the instruction is "if you sacrifice, you should begin doing good more than ever before." This I take to mean that the beginning and essential sacrifice is good-doing. This assumption is reinforced by the advice to release the objects of sacrifice and to renounce, and refrain from, i.e., give up, killing anything whatsoever (see Odu 70:1). Thus, the Kawaida tradition reads this and related texts as a divine preference for self-giving as distinct from object-giving, although it recognizes and respects the practice of sacrifice as object-giving in the historical and current Ifa tradition.

Also, Kawaida, which has embraced and expanded the understanding and practice of the ancient Egyptian Maatian tradition, finds additional support in it for moral self-giving. In this ancient African ethical tradition, doing *Maat*, i.e., right in the broadest sense, is the essential offering to the Divine. In the *Husia*, Kheti says, "make worthy your house in the West and make firm your place in God's domain by being upright and just. It is on this that the hearts of men and women rely. For more acceptable is the virtue of the righteous than the (sacrificed) ox of those who do evil." And Queen

Hatshepsut says to the Lord of Heaven, "I offer you *Maat* for I know you live by it." In a word, then, *Maat*, or *Ire* or *rere-ișe* (doing good and right) is the essential offering in the Kawaida tradition and it is how we read the Ifa tradition without denying the central meaning of the ritual sacrifice to it.

A second requirement for moving from an almost exclusive divination-focused reading of the Odu to an essentially ethics-focused reading is the need for an expanded interpretation of the phrase "*a dífá fún*." This phrase is usually translated as "divination was performed for" but may be translated in various other ways which stress divination. However, an ethical-focused interpretation of the texts requires that the interpretive dimension of divination and the text themselves be expanded so that the interpretation is not only of the signs but also of *the teachings of Ifa*. Thus, in Kawaida, we translate "*a dífá fún*" as "*the teachings of Ifa were interpreted for*" or "*this was the teaching of Ifa for.*" This allows for interpretations of both ethical and other instructions in matters of life and death, human problems and prospects, this-world and other-world concerns and considerations.

A final requirement for the transition from an almost exclusive divination-focused interpretation of the *Odu Ifa* to an essentially ethics-focused reading is the cultivation among scholars, priests and general adherents of a wide-reaching, thorough and profound ethical dialog tradition. In such a tradition, persons will engage the texts, personally and communally, as a fundamental source of the best of African and human ethics, constantly reading and re-reading them to discover and recover ancient and modern meaning in the ongoing quest to answer current moral questions, and to envision and bring into being the moral community, just society and good world we all want and deserve to live in. Thus, it will become and be for us a sacred legacy of moral instruction left by our ancestors and offered by us to the generations that follow. And this legacy will have at its core the ethical teaching and practice of speaking truth and doing justice, honoring elders and ancestors, caring for the vulnerable, having a rightful relation with the environment, resisting evil and constantly raising up and pursuing the good, in ever more expansive ways.

The Ethical Framework

A Kawaida reading of the Odu Ifa finds an ethics rooted in the four fundamental pillars of the larger African ethical tradition. These fundamental principles are respect for and commitment to: (1) the dignity and rights of the human person; (2) the well-being and flourishing of family and community; (3) the integrity and value of the environment; and (4) the reciprocal solidarity and common interests of humanity. The conceptual context for the evolution of Ifa ethics is a spirituality which conceives of the world as essentially good but constantly needing to be renewed, repaired and enriched with good. Secondly, humans are designed by the Creator as those chosen to constantly bring good into the world and not let any good be lost (Iwosu'wori, 78). This *chosenness*, along with its companion concept of being *ọmọ Olódùmarè*, the offspring of God, offer a ground for the ethical principle of human dignity or the inherent and inviolable worthiness of each and every human. The divine designiation of humans as chosen ones, *ènìyàn*, carries with it, not only a special status of beings with an inherent and inviolable worthiness. It also, as Odu Irosu'wori (78) tells us, suggests that the fundamental mission and meaning of human life is to constantly bring good into the world.

In order to achieve this ongoing task, as is explained in Odu Irosu'wori (78), humans are told that they need several essential attributes and virtues. These include: wisdom, character, the love of doing good, especially for the needy, and constant *commitment* and *struggle* to bringing good into the world and not let any good be lost. Likewise, we are told throughout the texts that we must be good parents, sons and daughters, friends and fellow human beings and that we should respect our elders and ancestors, with the understanding that our *togetherness in harmony* insures and enhances our ability to bring, give and receive good in the world. The principle here, as Odu Osa'gunda (202:1) tells us, is *àṣùwà*, gathering together in harmony for the good. In fact, the text says that "all good comes from the gathering together in harmony."

The Odu Ifa also reminds us of our obligation to the earth, indeed the world, and our reciprocal relationship with it. It urges us to avoid plundering, polluting and depleting the earth in our pursuit of wealth and comfort. Instead, Odu Osa Meji (10:5) urges us to *sacrifice* so that the integrity of the earth can be maintained and we can honor our reciprocal relationship with the world in which we live and are a part. For "in this way, we live" also. In conclusion, then, the moral imagination and instruction in the Odu Ifa are rich, varied and resourceful. And it is an ancient legacy worthy of the most profound reflection and the most serious practice in engaging in meaningful and beneficial ways the critical issues of our times.

Textual Notes

In preparing the translations, I have used the Epega model rather than the Fama model for ordering the minor Odu, although it's my understanding that each is valid. Our choice is based on the assumed greater antiquity of the Epega model, though the Fama model seems easier to learn and follow. I have also consciously made use of the gender neutrality which the Yoruba language offers in pronominal use of "he" and "she" to balance male/female representation in the text without trying to achieve an exact ratio of one-to-one. This is done first because faithfulness to the texts allows and often requires this. But it is also done to emphasize that the best of African ethics and spirituality recognizes the indispensability and equal value, role and responsibility of woman in the world as expressed in the Odu Osa Meji (10:2) and Ose Otura (248:1).

Also, in the interest of the scholarly and regular need for citation, the Odu are ordered so that one may cite Odu, *ẹsẹ* (verse) and line. This may be written, for example 248:1.1-2, meaning, Odu 248, verse 1, lines 1-2. Given that often a literal translation is neither clear nor the best, I have tried to translate the text in a way which reveals its capacity for an expanded imagery and message without sacrificing its literal or essential meaning. And where I've added a word or phrase to the text for clarity, I have used italics to signify this.

Moreover, I have offered commentaries, *àsọyé,* only on a selected number of Odu. This is not only because of the need to keep the text an accessible length, but also to allow as much as possible an uninterrupted reading of the text as a whole. Also, it is hoped that efforts to understand the text from our own personal and various group vantage points will enrich and expand the discourse around the text. My intention in providing the commentaries is simply to offer a useful framework for understanding and engaging the most essential concepts in this rich and inexhaustible storehouse of moral instruction and moral imagination. It is in this spirit of encouraging an ongoing and constantly expanding dialog around the ethical teachings of the Odu Ifa that the Kawaida Institute of Pan-African Studies (Us) has called and co-sponsored the Conference on Yoruba Culture and Ethics, "Ethics and Spirituality in the Odu Ifa: Bringing Good into the World," February 4-7, 1999 in Los Angeles. And it is also in pursuit and support of such a dialog that I have especially prepared this volume to be released and discussed at this conference.

The obvious stress on ethical teaching and learning represents the Kawaida rootedness in the African moral teacher or *Seba* tradition that reaches back to ancient Egypt. It is a tradition of which the Odu are a fundamental part according to our understanding. In the Kawaida tradition, Orunmila is, above all, a sage and an *Olùkọ́*, a teacher or more precisely an *Olùkọ́-ìwàrere*, a moral teacher. And here moral includes and necessitates the spiritual, i.e., commitment to the Transcendent. Thus, the stress on the ethical teachings of Ifa or Orunmila are central to our concept and translation of the text.

Obviously, then, I have edited the texts to focus in on the ethical teaching. This has produced Odu and verses of a few lines, as well as, Odu of whole narratives. Many of the texts collected originally reflected the dialectical variants of the areas or sources from which they came or in which they were recorded. As far as possible, I have tried to standardize the textual language, using standard Yoruba unless change of the word to its standard form proved impossible or unadvisable. As in my work in ancient Egyptian texts, I have tried to recapture in the Yoruba texts the poetic beauty of the moral imagination, imagery and instruction of the Odu Ifa.

We, at the Kawaida Institute of Pan-African Studies, have collected these texts from a wide range of sources, often a few texts or even one text from a series of single sources. But clearly the major collection of texts from early and current authors are the main source of the texts in this work, even though the Odu are sometimes duplicated in various sources and may have varied in text and dialect. We have approached the Odu Ifa itself as a common heritage of African people available for varied translations and interpretations while still respecting prior and other particular translations and interpretations as the protected intellectual work of each author. The model for this is the ability of interested persons to translate and interpret the other major religious texts collected by others such as the *Quran*, *Bible*, *Husia*, *Dhammapada*, *Torah*,

Bhaghavad-Gita, etc., without infringing on the rights of those who collected and/or assembled them. Thus, in preparing these translations and commentaries, I have used the existing original texts and benefitted from the early and current translations and studies of the Odu which, as mentioned above, are scattered throughout the literature.

Acknowledgements

My list of acknowledgments in this area is obviously and rightfully long. And a selected list of key sources follow at the end of the text. First, I am profoundly indebted to those who recorded this oral tradition in writing and began the dialog around and within the Ifa tradition: Babalawo Fagbenro Beyioku, Rev. E.M. Lijadu, Babalawo Fela Sowande and especially Rev. D. Onadele Epega who has provided us with the most complete corpus of Ifa texts and who founded the Imole Oluwa Institute for the studying and publishing of Ifa texts. Likewise, I have benefitted from the work of Babalawos Afolabi A. Epega, his grandson, and Philip Neimark for providing an English translation and commentary on this essential and extensive text; Iyanifa Aina Fama Adewale for her valuable work on the theological narratives of the Odu with accompanying Yoruba texts; Babalawo S. Solagbade Popoola for his insightful translations and interpretations of the Odu texts; Alagba David A. Adeniji and Dr. Akinsola Akiwowo for their invaluable work of collection and interpretation of the texts, especially the *Aláṣùwàdà* text of Osa'gunda; and William Bascom for his collection and commentary.

Certainly, I am greatly indebted to Dr. Wande Abimbola, the internationally renowned scholar of the Odu Ifa and Yoruba theology and culture whose seminal work in translation and in linguistic, poetic, textual, historical and cultural analysis of the Odu texts has been an invaluable source of knowledge for me. Moreover, he has given me valuable support and advice and has provided me with insightful and helpful reviews of both individual texts and this work as a whole. Such an interest in and encouragement of my work have special meaning, not only because of his intellectual status as preeminent authority on the Odu texts, but also because of his status as *Àwíṣẹ Àgbáyé* (spokesperson for Ifa in the world).

I owe thanks also to Dr. E. Bolaji Idowu whose work *Olodumare: God in Yoruba Belief* was my introduction to Yoruba religion and ethics and which I read while at UCLA in the midst of developing my philosophy, Kawaida, in the 60's. In fact, I taught from his book in *Mwalimu* class, a class for the training of moral teachers now called *Seba* in the Kawaida tradition. And I am sure the Yoruba stress on character as a personal and social value as discussed by him influenced greatly my focus on values as central to personal and collective practice in Kawaida philosophy. Likewise, I have benefitted greatly from the incisive interpretations of art, ethics and culture of Dr. Babatunde Lawal and Dr. Rowland Abiodun.

I reserve a special thanks for Dr. Stephen Adewole, an accomplished linguist and my first tutor in Yoruba, who offered important linguistic as well as cultural insights as we meticulously worked our way through the Odu. And thanks is also due to Dr. Yetunde Laniran, also a proficient linguist, who critically reviewed the final manuscript to insure the accuracy of diacritical marks and standardization of the language. A special thanks goes also to Dr. Molefi Asante, a colleague of the first rank whose continuous discussion of African culture with me is always engaging and valuable.

As always, I give the greatest thanks to the members of my organization Us who provide me with the support and intellectual challenge and exchange indispensable to this and other of my projects, especially to Thabiti Ambata, Tulivu Jadi, Tukufu Kalonji, Thanayi Karenga, Tiamoyo Karenga, Mpinduzi Khuthaza, MHimili Kinamo, Mshinda Nyofu, Aminisha Tambuzi, Robert Tambuzi, Mark Tangulifu, Chimbuko Tembo, Limbiko Tembo and Ujima Wema. Moreover, I am grateful to the members of the National Association of Kawaida Organizstions (NAKO), especially those in New

York, Philadelphia, and Chicago who have also provided me with an important context of support and exchange. My gratitude is also special and continuing to my publishers and friends, Chimbuko Tembo and Limbiko Tembo, whose involvement in my creative projects are always supportive, sustained and greatly helpful.

As ever, there is no greater debt I owe or thanks I can give than that which I owe and give to my friend, wife and companion in all things good, pure and eternal, Tiamoyo Karenga. It is she who is always my first and final collaborator and colleague, my typist, proofreader, editor and co-creator of the good. I bear the burden of my own mistakes, but any good which comes from this and other works surely is shared with all those who made them possible. May the ancestors who gave us these texts on the good and the right and who opened the way to the good society and world for us, be pleased with our efforts and our humble offerings. *Aṣẹ*.

Maulana Karenga
Professor and Chair, Department of Black Studies
California State University, Long Beach

Kawaida Institute of Pan-African Studies
Los Angeles, California

ODÙ IFÁ
THE ETHICAL TEACHINGS

ÈJÌ OGBÈ

ODÙ 1

1:1

Let us not engage the world hurriedly.
Let us not grasp at the rope of wealth
impatiently.
That which should be treated with mature
judgment,
Let us not deal with in a state of
uncontrolled passion.
When we arrive at a cool place,
Let us rest fully.
Let us give continuous attention to the future.
Let us give deep consideration to the
consequences of things.
And this because of our eventual passing.

K'á má fi kánjúkánjú j'ayé.
K'á má fi wàràwàrà n'okùn ọrọ̀.
Ohun a bá fi ṣ'àgbá,
K'á má fi ṣè'bínú.
Bí a bá dé'bi t'ó tútù,
K'á simi-simi.
K'á wò'wajú ọjọ́ lọ títí.
K'á tún bọ̀ wá r'ẹ̀hìn ọ̀ràn wò.
Nítorí àti sùn ara ẹni ni.

1 : 1

ÀSỌYÉ

This is a teaching on having a measured approach to achieving the good life. It reflects the Odu stress on the virtue of *ìwọ̀n,* or balance, and the *amúwọ̀n*, the balanced person. We are not to engage the world in a hurried, heedless or reckless manner. Nor are we to seek material gain impatiently. For although Odu ethics poses wealth as one of the main blessings in life as well as an important condition to live a truly full life and a means to aid and share with others, there is continuous concern that pursuit of material gain not be excessive or all-consuming (Odu, 82:1). The good or moral life, the teaching tells us, also necessitates that we treat important matters with the reasonableness and calmness they require.

Moreover, the text suggests that the good life also requires that we know when and how to rest. It poses rest as an essential condition not only for the good life in general, but also specifically for serious moral and critical reflection. Finally, the text tells us that we should give full and ongoing attention to the future and be constantly and profoundly concerned about the consequences of things. This dual moral emphasis speaks to our need to be concerned with the effect of our actions, not only on the quality of life and relations in the contemporary world, but also on the future of the world and generations to come. And thus, it has particular moral meaning not only for the quality of human relations, but for the integrity of the environment (Odu, 10:5).

Such moral concern, the text suggests, is to be embraced not only for the good life here, but also to secure our place in eternity given our eventual passing. In a word, it speaks to our need to live a life that leaves a legacy of goodness in this world which not only promises respectful memory in this world but also eternal life in the next.

1:2

Orunmila says it should be done little by little.
I say it is little by little we eat the head of the fish.
We are not as large as the elephant nor as sturdy as the buffalo.
The sash worn underneath is not equal to the sash tied on top.
No noble is as great as the Oni of Ife.
No string of cowries is as long as that of Yemideregbe.
Yemideregbe is what we call the owner of the sea.
Orunmila says that we should measure the length and measure the breadth of things.
The hand reaches much higher than the head.
And the young palm fronds extend much higher than the old palm fronds.
But no forest is so dense that the iroko tree cannot be seen.
And no celebration is so loud that the gong cannot be heard.

1:2

Òrúnmìlà ní ó di kẹ́rẹ́kẹ́rẹ́.
Èmi ní kẹ́rẹ́kẹ́rẹ́ l'àá j'orí ẹja.
A kí igbà tobi t'erin, a kí sẹ yẹ̀kẹ̀tẹ̀ t'ẹ́fọ̀n.
Ọ̀já kí it' ọ́ja igba lé.
Elú k'élú kí it' Ọ́ni Ife.
Okún owó ẹyọ kí it'ókùn Yemideregbe.
Yemideregbe l'orúkọ a p'ólókun.
Ọ̀rúnmìlà ni k'á wọ̀n n'ìbú k'á wòn n'ìró.
Gbọgbọrọgbọ l'ọwọ́ yọ j'orí.
Gbọgbọrọgbo ni màrìwò ọ̀pẹ yọ j'ọgọmọ
Igbó kí'dí kí ìrókò kí ó má yọ.
A kí ik'eré jọ kí t'agogo kí ó má yọ.

1:2

ÀSỌYÉ

This is a teaching on moderation in our approach to life and in our truthful evaluation of our ability, potential and possibilities. Things should be done "little by little" or "step by step," the text tells us. For such a measured approach enables us to make adequate evaluations in our engagement and understanding of things. In a word, the text says, "We should measure the length and breadth of things." This also implies our need to delve into the depth of things. For the metaphor of the sash underneath of the one on top requires our going below the surface to see difference and distinction. And, indeed, the examination of each situation itself, requires depthful reflection.

This verse also teaches that even though we must not overestimate ourselves, we still must determine our possibilities, pursue them and make our own distinct contribution to the whole. Thus, we may not be as large as an elephant or sturdy as a buffalo, but we each have our own strengths. We are not the king of Ife; nor do we have the riches of the sea, but there is royalty in righteousness and riches in good character. And if we are not intellectually inclined, we must still use our heads the way we can and find the higher work our hands can reach and do.

Moreover, the teaching suggests that there are advantages to being both young and old. The old palm fronds have defined and strengthened the tree, but the young palm fronds, building on that base, must find their meaning in pushing forward further and higher. And finally, the text teaches that in the midst of the many, the distinct, by definition, stands out. Thus, no matter how dense the forest is, the iroko or African teak tree will still stand out and regardless of the loudness of the celebration, the gong dares to be heard.

In conclusion, we must approach life and the things before us in a measured and reflective way. And we must not be immobilized or dispirited by what we cannot do or be, but rather we must discover and clear our own paths of possibilities and pursue them.

1:3

Daylight does not endure beyond its usual
time.
Night does not last beyond its regular limit.
And darkness does not continue beyond
what is customary.
He who provides a pair of sandals for a
child's feet
Interpreted the teachings of Ifa for Baalejo
who was coming from heaven to earth.
If we have a problem,
We should take it to our ancestors.
He will protect us;
Our paternal ancestor will never desert us.
She will protect us;
Our maternal ancestor will never neglect us.
They will protect us;
Our Ifa teachings will never forsake us.
It shall protect us;
Our Ori, our inner head, will not abandon us.

1:3

Ọ̀sán ni ò sán pẹ́.
Òru ni ò ru pẹ́.
Òkùnkùn ò kùn pẹ́.
Ọ̀ pa bàtà m'ọmọ lẹ́sẹ̀ pẹ́ẹ́ pẹ̀ẹ̀ pẹ́ẹ́
A dífá fún Báalẹ̀jọ́
Tí nt' Ìkòlé ọ̀run bọ̀ wáyé.
Bá a bá lẹ̀jọ́ o,
Ṣe b'ọ́rún ẹni là á báá sọ.
Yóó gbè ọ́ o.
Baba ẹni kì í gbe'ni í tì.
Yóó gbè ọ́ o.
Iye ẹni kì í gbe'ni í tì.
Yóó gbè ọ́ o.
Ìkín ẹni kì í gbe'ni í tì.
Yóó gbè ọ́ o.
Orí ẹni kì í gbe'ni í tì.

1:3

ÀSỌYÉ

This Odu focuses first on the lesson that we should be knowledgeable on how the world works and have enough patience to see it unfold. It suggests that night and day become unbearably long for the impatient or anxious person, but the wise and self-controlled person sits down calmly, as the ancient Egyptian says, anticipating what happens, knowing what will occur.

Also, the text teaches that we have no real reason to worry unduly. Caution against injury, Odu 222:2 says, is not being overly fearful, for we must defend ourselves. Here the answer is spiritual and moral grounding through linking with the ancestors and, by extension, following in their ways. The portrait of a caring Creator is immediately projected by his praise name, "He who provides a pair of sandals (even) for a child's feet." And the way of the ancestors which is always and infinitely moral and spiritual is key to how well we walk and prosper in the world. Thus, the advice of the Odu is take our problems to our maternal and paternal ancestors, study the ways and teachings of Ifa, and honor the council of the inner, the divinely-placed guide and ground in all of us.

ÈJÌ OGBÈ

I

1:4

If a friend is exceedingly kind,
He is like a relative of one's mother or father.
Ifa says that one who seeks a new friend
Will find that friend to be of great value.

B' ọ́rẹ́ bá nínúrere l'à nínúrere jù,
Á dàbí ìyékan.
Ifá ní eni tí ńfé ni ọ́rẹ́ titun kan
Ọ̀rẹ́ náà yíò ṣe ní ànfààní ńlá.

1:4

ÀSỌYÉ

Here this Odu reaffirm the social basis of relationships. The friend who is exceedingly kind is described as "*dàbí ìyékan*" or a person who resembles a relative of one's parents. Clearly, we are not talking about physical similarity here but moral and spiritual resemblance, i.e., loving, kind, giving, protective, a bringer of good. Inherent in this brief *ẹsẹ̀* or verse is that message that friendship has a special place in Yoruba social and ethical life. Many of the ethical teachings measure the quality of our ethical commitments and ethical life by our relationship with our friends. Injunctions are throughout the texts on loving and helping of friends, on speaking truth and doing justice to them, not betraying them or seducing their partners.

The text encourages us to seek new friends, saying we will find them of great value--indeed, of great value in every sense of the word. And this is so not only in the sense of support, creative challenge and the joy of sharing, but also by serving in the role of mirror and honest advisor in the midst of our constant growth and development. As for others, we might find reasons to reject their advice. But with friends, we are obligated to listen.

1:5

I lift up my arms and walk in joyful
satisfaction.
This was the teaching of Ifa for Orunmila.
They said Baba would not be able to carry
out his responsibilities to the end
of his life.
But I will carry out my responsibilities to
the end of my life.
And so, I lift up my arms and walk with
dignity and measured movement.

Mo ṣípá; mo yan gede.
A dífá fún Ọ̀rúnmìlà.
Wọ́n ní Baba ò ní lè rẹrù rẹ̀ dalẹ́.
Èmi nìkán ni n ó rẹrù mi dalẹ́.
Mo sípá; mo yan gede.

1:5

ÀSỌYÉ

This is a teaching on the joyful acceptance and carrying out of our responsibilities of life. The teaching begins with the teacher declaring that he will lift up his arms in joyful satisfaction of carrying out his responsibilities. He notes the sentiment that Baba, meaning Orunmila, will not carry out his responsibilities to the end of his life. But we who know Orunmila will indeed carry out his responsibilities. For throughout the Odu, the text tells us that he will not move or be moved by the seductions of money and material things, sex, comfort or power. He is the master teacher of Ifa, the good life, witness to creation and he cannot be diverted or dispirited.

The verse turns to each of us and gives us a chance to answer a question inherent in the discussion: will we carry out your responsibilities to the rest of our life? This question, of course, raises the related question of what kind of responsibilities? And the Odu reveal both grand and specific responsibilities. We are first of all reminded by Odu 78 that we are chosen by the Divine to bring good into the world; that we should let no good be lost; and finally, that we should do our work and live our lives with joy. Specifically and within the framework of this moral guideline, the Odu instruct us to speak truth, do justice, care for the vulnerable and needy, honor and care for the elders, raise our children right, relate rightfully to the world around us, and again do it with a triumphant sense of joy.

ÒYẸ̀KÚ MÉJÌ
2

2:1

Constantly shifting is a boat on water.
And so are human beings.
This was the teaching of Ifa for Ona Ishokan
Who was a child of the King of Oyo.
One who is brave
Should not assume the voice of the timid.
And one who is timid
Should not talk like one who is brave.
The king does not allow us to make war on a
town of women
So that we may go with them.
Let us conduct ourselves with gentleness
So that we may pass peacefully,
And so that our children can stretch forth
their hands fully
On us in burial.

ÒYẸ̀KÚ MÉJÌ
2

2:1

Bíríbírí l'ọkọ̀ dá.
Bẹ̀ẹ̀náni ni ọmọ aráyé.
A dífá fún Ọ̀nà Ìṣọ̀kun
Tí iṣe ọmọ ọba l'óde Ọ̀yọ́.
Ẹnití ó bá ńs'akin
K'ó má m'óhùn ojo.
Ẹnití ó bá nṣ'ojo
K'ó má m'óhùn akin.
Ọba kò jẹ́kí á ṣ'ogun sí ìlú obirin,
K'á bá wọ́n lọ.
K'ẹni hùwà gbẹ̀dẹ̀gbẹ̀dẹ̀
K'ẹni lè kú pẹ̀lẹ́ pẹ̀lẹ́.
K'ómọ ẹni lè n'ọ́wọ́ gbogbogbo
L'ẹni sin.

2:1

ÀSỌYÉ

This is a teaching on the virtues of genuineness, gentleness and truthful self-presentation. It begins by recognizing that human beings are in a constant process of change, i.e., "constantly shifting" from one place, position, level of development, etc., to another. The implicit challenge here, then, becomes one of always being one's real self in the midst of the demands of change. The text also teaches that a person should neither hide one's courage nor pretend a courage one does not have. The courageous are compelled to step forward and the timid are counseled to be modest in their claims. This teaching is important in stressing the need for those who are capable to always show moral courage as well as courage of heart and mind in difficult situations when it would be easy to step back, remain silent or "assume the voice of the timid." The counsel here is to not disguise oneself and by extension to stand up and step forward in the service of good (*ire*). On the other hand, the verse counsels the timid not to pretend courage but to strengthen themselves through self-development and practice which leads to the acquisition of courage.

Likewise, the text suggests that the example of the coward posing as a courageous person is found in men who would "make war on" or attack women in various ways to have access to and control of them. The teaching is that in a group situation, a real ruler or leader would not permit it and that the moral path to access and exchange is through gentlesness. "We are to behave gently then" to achieve our ends in the world.

The last part of this Odu, then, is a teaching on gentleness of behavior. It advises us to be gentle in all we do. And although there are numerous other reasons given in the Odu for being gentle, this *esè* gives two main ones. The first reason this verse gives for our need to be gentle is so "that we might leave life peacefully," that is to say, so that we may die *at peace* and *in peace*. To die or pass *at peace* is to pass into the next world without undue worry about what will be left behind or what will be met ahead. And to die or pass *in peace* is to lie down to make the transition to the next world in the midst of harmony, love, calmness, contentment and untroubleness. In a word, it is to leave life in a moral community we ourselves have helped create.

The second reason the text gives us for behaving gently in life is so that our children who experience this loving kindness will reciprocate and respond to our passing in a loving and respectful manner. The teaching tells us that we must live our lives in a manner which causes love and respect from our children which in turn causes them "to stretch forth their hands fully upon us," that is to say, to embrace us fully in death as they did in life.

In sum, then, to leave life peacefully is to act in life with such gentle kindness that we leave a legacy of goodness in this world which is the basis for respectful memory in this world and eternal life in the next.

ÒYÈKÚ MÉJÌ
2

2:2

Let us not lie against a companion.
Let us not break a commitment to an
associate.
And this, because of our eventual passing.

K'á má ṣ'èké ẹgbẹ́.
K'á má da'lẹ̀ ọ̀gbà.
Nítorí àti sùn ara eni ni.

Ọ̀YẸ̀KÚ MÉJÌ
2

2:2

ÀSỌYÉ

This is a teaching on not lying against or to a friend, companion or an associate, or breaking a commitment one makes to another. The emphasis is on truth-telling and commitment-keeping as essential to friendship and by extension to all relations of closeness. Surely, these two values are essential in any relationship, but they take on added meaning in close relations like friendship or companionship. The importance of avoiding such behavior is underlined by the verse's reminding us of our mortality and the need to live in such a way that our passing is a good one. That is to say, that it is peaceful in this life and promising in the next.

It is important to note that Ifa ethics uses *ọ̀rẹ́*, friend, or similar categories of closeness, i.e., *ẹgbé* (companion, comrade) or *ògbà* (associate, peer), rather than *aládugbò*, neighbor, to teach moral lessons and moral practice of respect and concern for others. The moral reasoning concerning this seems to be that human solidarity is best achieved in the quest for and practice directed toward friendship. Likewise, the violation of a friendship, even more than a similar injury to a neighbor, reveals the gravity of the moral offense. My sense is that a neighbor requires much less of us. We may and often do keep a respectful distance from most neighbors, tolerating some and actually hating others. But friends, real friends, are here, as in the ancient Egyptian and Kawaida tradition, a mirror and map of the best of what we can become as an African and human being.

This does not mean that friends cannot and do not sometimes injure or even betray us. But the value of friendship, the text suggests, outweighs any risks such a relationship might bring.

2:3

Ifa says that a visitor is coming
And that we should take care of her
Lest her kindness and goodness pass us by.
For there is value in the presence of a visitor.

Ifá ní àlejó kan ńbọ̀
K'á tọ́jú rẹ̀,
Kí oore àti ire rẹ̀ má bá kọjá ẹni
Nítorí ànfààní wá l'ára àlejó náà.

Ifa says that a stranger is coming
And that we should take care of him,
Lest his kindness and goodness pass us by.
For there is value in the presence of a stranger.

2:3

ÀSỌYÉ

This verse focuses on the moral considerability of the guest or stranger. Like many other African languages, Yoruba uses the same word, "*àlejó*" for both stranger and guest. For example in Swahili, Zulu and ancient Egyptian, the words "*mgeni*," "*isihambi*," and "*kri*" may mean visitor or stranger. This suggests a positive approach to the stranger which welcomes him or her as a guest as distinct from a xenophobic response which sees the stranger as threat or enemy. Clearly, in the Maatian ethics of ancient Egypt the moral considerability of the stranger is a basic principle. Thus, in the *Husia*, the stranger is to be welcomed, and we read assertions that one was kind and generous to those whom one did not know like those whom one did know.

The key point here is that in many African societies, the considerability of the stranger is a central element in the moral calculus of the right, the wrong and the worthy, and in Yoruba culture counts among these. In this verse, the moral assumption is made that the stranger brings something of good and value and we risk losing it by not welcoming and taking good care of him or her.

The issue of possible vulnerability from too quick or too close an embrace of a stranger speaks to the virtues of balance and reciprocity found throughout the Odu Ifa. The first virtue teaches us to be balanced in all things. Here a balance of heart (moral sensitivity) and head (social reasoning informed by moral sensitivity) are central. One presumes, then, that the other is a potential good neighbor and possible friend until actions prove otherwise. And one never invests beyond what is warranted by reciprocal response. Such a posture becomes an important way to avoid vulnerability to exploitation and injury on one hand and unwarranted hostility on the other.

2:4

Even if you move away from your position,
I will not move.
The foundation stones of the house must not fail the house.
And the crown of the head must not fail the person at the market.
So I will not move away.
And you will not move away.
Twilight is just appearing in the heavens,
But some people thought day had already dawned.
This was the teaching of Ifa for Eji Oye
Who would dawn on earth like daylight.
So, if it were money that moved me,
I would certainly say so.
But Ifa will assign me my own good fortune.

2:4

Bí o bá yẹ̀.
Èmi ò yẹ̀.
Yangi ilé, wọn ò gbọdọ̀ yẹlẹ́.
Àtàrí, wọn ò gbọdọ̀ yẹ èrò ọjà.
Èmi ò yẹ̀.
Ìwọ ò yẹ.
Òyẹ̀ ṣẹ̀ṣẹ̀ ńlá bọ̀ lókè,
Wọ́n ṣe bójúmó ní ńmọ́.
A dífá f'Éjì Ọ̀yẹ̀
Tí ó t'ojú ọ̀run là wáyé bí ọ̀bẹ̀rẹ̀kẹ̀.
Njẹ́ owó ló bá ńwú mì,
Dandan, mo wí.
Ifá ni ó yẹ're tèmi f'émi.

2:4

ÀSỌYÉ

This verse stresses the virtue of steadfastness in the right and the good. It promises that such a commitment to the way of Ifa, the way of rightness, will bring a good fortune beyond material gains. Moreover, the teaching invites us to see the virtue of steadfastness as essential to maintaining the good in the world as the foundation stones of the house are to upholding it and as useful to a person as the crown of the head is to one in the market who uses the head on which to carry heavy and valuable loads.

The verse begins by declaring a commitment to hold firm to the position of the good and right even if others move away from it. But it also expresses a moral optimism in others by declaring however that "I will not move away and you will not move away." This suggests not only a genuine moral optimism about the human will to hold to the good, but perhaps also suggests our constant need to support others in their struggle to keep their position. Also, important in this teaching is the subtle lesson that people are often drawn from their positions of steadfastness in the right by misreading signs of achievement or change. Thus, it says although it was only twilight which was appearing in the heavens, some thought it was already daylight and apparently acted accordingly. The sense seems to be that they, misreading the situations, moved away from their positions prematurely, like those in struggle misreading the turn of events, assuming victory before the battle is won and walking away from the battlefield.

Finally, the text also suggests that material gain, here in the form of money, can also entice us to leave the way and lose the way. But the assertion is that if we don't confuse money or material gain with the good fortune Ifa offers, we will gain a special good and be among those who will, through steadfastness in the good and right, "dawn on earth like daylight."

2:5

Fierce is the fire on the face of those who gather honey.
Severe is the sun on the bent back of the farmer.
The one who gathers honey suffers losses;
The honey bee moves away and the honey is eventually exhausted.
But the house of the teacher of Ifa is never empty.
Ifa says he will not allow us to come up empty-handed
In that for which we seek the advice of Ifa.

Iná kankan ni'wájú arẹ́yin.
Oòrún kankan n'íbàdí àgbẹ̀.
Ti arẹ́yin á di ègbé.
Oyin sí àti àdó rẹ̀.
Ṣùgbọ́n ilé awo kò ní gb'ófo.
Ifá ní òun kò ń jẹ́kí a pòfo.
Ni ohun tí a dá Ifá.

2:5

ÀSỌYÉ

This is an ese in praise of the rewards of studying Ifa and following the counsel of the Odu. It tells us that the gathering of the sweet of honey brings with it the heat from the fire used to smoke out the bees and that the sun is severe on the back of farmers as they works the fields for their yield. These examples teach us to recognize that good gain requires sacrifice and effort. But then the gathering of honey as a problematic, questionable and ephemeral gain is contrasted with the counsel of Ifa as a sure and lasting good.

This verse complements the previous and following verses which praise the power and promise of our study and practice of the teachings of Ifa. Also, it reaffirms the need to hold on to what the ancient Egyptians called "that which endures in the midst of that which is overthrown," i.e., our moral and spiritual principles which give direction, meaning and fullness to our lives. And the way of Ifa is clearly and certainly the central source and ground of these principles in these texts.

2:6

Orunmila says there should be a gathering
together like trees do to form a forest.
I say there should be a gathering together.
We find monkeys in groups.
We find wild pigs in groups.
We don't even find "one who keeps silent"
walking alone.
Nor do we find the greedy one walking alone.
Ifa says we should gather together and not
walk alone.

Ọ̀rúnmìlà ní ó bá di igbó.
Mo ní ó di bá igbó ni.
Igbó ni àá bá ehan.
Igbó ni àá bá esi.
A kí rí anìkarìn nadunadu.
A kí rì anìkarìn yunrẹ̀.
Ifá ní a bá di igbó, kò sì n'ọ̀kan rin.

ÌWÒRÌ MÉJÌ

3

3: 1

Orunmila says we should cry "watch out!"
I say "One who is in the way should move
to the side."
He says "We should look before we throw
out water,
So that we don't throw water on a stranger."
I ask "what stranger?"
He says, "a visitor who brings fortune,
a spouse, children, or honor."
Ifa says that he sees the blessings of visitors.
The blessing of fortune, the blessing of a
spouse, the blessings of children,
and the blessing of honor.

ÌWÒRÌ MÉJÌ

3

3:1

Ọ̀rúnmìlà ní ó di "sìì."
Mo ní "k'ó ró yẹ̀'ba."
Ó ní "k'á ṣó omi dà.
K'á má bá da omí si àlejò l'ára."
Mo ní "àlejò wo ni?"
Ó ní "àlejò ajé, aya tàbí ọkọ, ọmọ àti oyè ni".
Ifá ní òún rí ire àlejò.
Ire ajé, ire aya tàbí ọkọ àti ire oyè.

3:2

If a young person shows deference to an elder,
Everything he attempts to do
Will turn out exactly right.
And he will be extremely serene of character.
This was the teaching of Ifa for the young
person of gentle character
Who did not disrespect his mother or father
And whose life was exceedingly pleasant.

Bí ọmọdé bá tẹríba fún àgba,
Ohun gbogbo tí ó bá dáwọ́lé,
Á má gún gẹ́gẹ́gẹ́.
Ìwá rè á sì má tutù pẹ̀sẹ̀ pẹ̀sẹ̀.
A dífá f'ọmọ oníwà pẹ̀lẹ́
Tí kò ṣe àfojúdi sí ìyá tàbí baba
Ti ayé rẹ̀ dùn jọjọ.

ÒDÍ MÉJÌ
4

4:1

I arrive well.
I travel well.
I am one who usually travels and finds fortune.
Just as they were laying down riches,
I entered without hesitation like an offspring
of the owner
But I am not an offpsring of the owner.
I am only one who knows how to travel
And find good fortune.

Mo dé rere.
Mo rín rere.
Èmi nìkan ni mo mọ̀ rin àrìnkòórìn.
A ṣèṣè ńkóhun ọrọ̀ sìlẹ̀,
Ni mo wọlẹ̀ wẹ́rẹ́ bí omo olọ́hun.
Èmi èé ṣ'ọmọ olọ́hun.
Ìrìn àrìnkò ni mo mọ̀ọ́ rìn.

4:1

ÀSỌYÉ

This Odu teaches us the virtue of expecting and finding good wherever we go. It says that to travel well and to arrive well enables or leads one to find good fortune. The text suggests that central to traveling and arriving well is a positive attitude that expects and finds good in the world. It also suggests that when we find good in the world we should boldly and confidently reach out to embrace it and share in it. This is the meaning of the line that says the person in the text "entered without hesitation like the offspring of the owner." But as the person says, s/he was not the owner's offspring, only "one who knows how to travel and find good fortune.

Again the central lesson here is that finding fortune or goodness in the world begins with a positive attitude, a necessary sense of possibility and culminates with a bold and confident self-assertion at the right moment to embrace and share the good of the world. And this, of course, is a reaffirmation of the sense of human agency which is so central to Odu ethics and spirituality.

ÒDÍ MÉJÌ

4

4:2

You arrive well.
You travel well.
You know how to walk on foot and
still be on time.
Just when the valuables are being layed out
on the ground
You arrive just like you were an offspring
of the owner.
This was the teaching of Ifa for the
important stranger,
Who was on his way to Benin City.
They said that someone's head would
bring him to a place
Where he would achieve his destiny
They said that in this very place, good things
will be accomplished.

4:2

They said he should sacrifice and
he heard and complied.
When he arrived in Benin, everything he
touched turned into something good.
Ifa says one who wants to go on a journey
should sacrifice.
So that s/he may gain honor, respect and wealth
at the place where s/he is going,
And so that there s/he may reap great rewards.

4:2

O dé rere.
O rìn rere.
O mò ìrìn asiko rìn l'ẹsẹ̀ méjèèjì.
A ṣẹ̀ṣẹ̀ kó ohun ọrọ̀ sílè,
O dé gẹ́gẹ́ bí ọmọ oníhun.
A dífá fún ájèjì gòdògbò
Tí lọ sí òde Ìbíní.
Wọ́n ní orí ẹníkan yìó múu dé ibití
Yìó gbé ṣe ìwà kan
Wọ́n ní ọ̀gangan ire ni yìó máa ṣe.
Wọ́n ní ó rúbọ; o gbọ́ ó rúbọ.
Nígbátí ó dé òde Ìbíní, ohunkóhun
ó bá fi ọwọ́ rè kan ni ó ndi rere.
Ifá ní ẹníkan tí ó nfé lọ sí ìdálẹ̀
kí mú ara kí ó rúbọ.
Kí ó bá lè rí ọlá, iyì àti ọrọ̀ ibití ó nlọ náà
Áti pé kí ìbé kí ó lè san dáradára.

4:3

May we not die young.
May we not reach an old age in wretchedness.
And may we not have to walk around with a stick
Searching for food at the place of sacrifice.

K'á má kú ni kékeré.
K'á má d'àgbàlágbà òsì.
K'á má f'ọ̀pá tà ilẹ̀
Ní 'bi ìjẹ ẹbọ.

4:3

ÀSỌYÉ

This is a teaching on expectations concerning reaching an old age. It presupposes that one has lived a moral life and can thus legitimately or justifiably expect goodness to come from this. Thus, the first expectation is that the person of character or good person will indeed reach an old age and not die young. This speaks to the conception of dying young as a greater tragedy than dying a ripe old age. For to pass young without having lived a full and meaningful life seems so meaningless in the scheme of things.

The second expectation is that the good person will not reach old age in a state of wretchedness. The category *òṣì* used in the text may mean misery, poverty or the general state characterized by distress, misery and lowliness which is translated here as wretchedness. This expectation is also, then, that we will die in dignity and not be left to waste away in pain, misery, poverty and the like. The third expectation of the person of character (*ìwà*) is that s/he will not have to look for food at the place of *ẹbọ* or sacrifice. This may mean the place of making sacrifices or the place of feasting tied to sacrificing.

These expectations are rooted both in the Yoruba and general African belief about how the divine works and how society and family should preform. Old age is a status of honor and deference in the family and society and thus the teaching is an indirect reminder to family and community of their obligation of care and responsibility of the aged.

4:4

The buttocks are sufficient support for a
person to sit on.
This was the teaching of Ifa for the gatekeeper
of the city of Ajengbere Mogun.
Who would stay in one place and there find
all good things.
There was no kind of work that the gatekeeper
had not done.
But he did not remain long in the same place.
Could he find fortune in this way?
This is the question he sought the answer
to from Ifa.
It was said that he should practice sacrifice.
And he practiced sacrifice.
After he practiced sacrifice,
It happened that when farmers arrived
from their farms
And when artisans returned from their travels,

Òdí Méjì

4

4:4

They gave the gatekeeper various kinds of
products like corn and yams.
After the gatekeeper had eaten and sufficiently
satisfied himself
He would then sell the rest of the products
It is in this way that the gatekeeper became a
rich man *by staying in the same place.*

4:4

Ìdi méjèèjí tó oúwarẹ̀ jókòó.
A díá f'óníbodè Ajẹ̀ngbẹ̀rẹ̀ Mògún.
Èyítí óò gbóju kan ríire gbogbo.
Kòsí iṣẹ́ tí oníbodè ò ṣe tán,
Òkan ò pé e níbè.
Òún lè ríre báyìí.
Ni oníbodè dáfá sí.
Wọ́n ní ẹbọ ní ó wá rú.
Ò sí rú u.
Igbà ó rúbọ tán,
Ló bá di pé bólóko ńtoko bọ̀,
Bọlọna ńtọ̀nà bọ̀,
Wọ́n ńfún oníbodè ni oríṣìríṣì nǹkan
bí àgbàdo àti iṣu.
Bóníbodè bá jẹ tó yó tan.
A sì tún tà nínú nnkan wọ̀nyi
Bẹ́ẹ̀ ni oníbodè ṣe tí ó fi dolówó.

ÌROSÙN MÉJÌ
5

5:1

After Orisha had married this certain woman,
He was afraid because it was said that
another person would take her from him.
So he built his house on a road at the back of
a walled courtyard.
And whenever anyone passed,
He began to suspect that perhaps someone
would take her from him.
Then the people began to sing:
"The noon day ripens quickly into heat waves;
And one who seeks trouble will find it."

Ìrosùn Méjì
5

5:1

Nígbàtí òrìṣà gbà obìrin yìí tán,
Ẹ́rú ńbàá nítorí tí ó wípé ẹlòmíràn
Yìó gbà ní ọwọ́ òun.
Nítorínáà ó lọ kọ́ ilé rẹ̀ sí ọ̀nà àgbàlá.
Nígbàkúúgbà tí ènìyàn bá ńkọjá níbẹ̀,
Ara á bẹ̀rẹ̀ sí fun òrìṣà pé bóyá
Ẹnìkan yìó tún gba òun ní ọwọ́ rẹ̀.
Nígbà náà ni wọ́n wa fi dá'rin pé:
"Ọ̀sán pọ́n wéréwéré;
Ẹni ó fín'dan á rí'dan."

Ọ̀WỌ́NRÍN MÉJÌ

6

6:1

It is stone which breaks suddenly
without bleeding.
This is the teaching of Ifa interpreted for Hand,
Offspring of one who inherits five fingers
and retains all five.
Hand was asked to sacrifice for her children
Because of the threat of death.
Hand performed sacrifice for all her five children,
And all the children survived.
She said "Hand's children should not die in
the presence of Hand.
Foot's children should not die in the presence
of Foot.
Very soon, at no distant date,
Come and find us alive, strong and healthy then."

Ọ̀WỌ́NRÍN MÉJÌ

6

6:1

Ọ̀kúta là pàá mọ́ ṣẹ̀jẹ̀
A dífá f'Ọ́wọ́.
Ọmọ abárúnjàrún
Wọ́n ní ó rúbọ fún ọmọ rẹ̀
Nítorí ikú.
Gbogbo ọmọ máràárún tí Ọ̀wọ
Bí náà ló rúbọ fún.
Gbogbo àwọn ọmọ náà sì yè
Ó ní, "ọmọ Ọwọ kì í t'ojú Ọwọ́ kú.
Ọmọ Ẹsẹ̀ kì í t'oju Ẹṣẹ̀ rọ̀run.
Kèè pẹ́ o,
Kèè jìnà,
Ẹ tètè wáá bá ni láìkú kangiri'."

Ọ̀KÀNRÀN MÉJÌ

8

8:1

If the host does not invite one to the
ceremony,
It is not proper to participate in it.
An improper practice causes a stern and
shameful face.
This was the teaching of Ifa for Eji Okanran,
Who was going to the city of Itile
May he just be allowed to walk in peace.
May he be permitted to walk with dignity.

Bélẹ́bọ ò pe ni,
Àsèfín ò yẹ ni.
Ọ̀ràn tí ò sunwọ̀n.
Konko ńṣojú.
A dífá fún Èjì Ọ̀kànràn,
Tí ńrelé Ìtilẹ̀.
Ẹ̀ sáà jẹ́ ó mọ́ọ rìn.
Ẹ̀ jé ó mọ́ọ yàn.

8:2

Thunder does not crash during the dry season;
Lightning does not flash in secret.
Male and female partridges do not have upright combs on their heads.
This was the teaching of Ifá for black Ereje, the mother of Agbo, the Ram;
She who had given birth to Erin, the Elephant, and to Efon, the Buffalo,
And likewise gave birth to Agbo, the Ram, as her third child.
When Shango, the spirit of Thunder, roared at Elephant and Buffalo,
They fled into the forest.
But when Shango roared at Agbo, the Ram,
This same ram roared right back at him.
He would not run; he fought with Shango, the spirit of thunder,

8:2

After they had struggled for a while,
Shango withdrew and returned to heaven.
Since that time, Shango, the spirit of Thunder,
remains in heaven.
And whenever the thunder roars and the
lightning flashes.
Agbo, the Ram, paws the ground and says:
"Our fight is not finished yet."

8:2

Ọyẹ́ kò sán ààrá;
Mọ̀nàmọ́ná kò jírẹrẹ kọ
Akọ àparò àti abo àparò kò là ogbe l'órí ṣanṣan
A dífá fún Erejẹ dúdú, yèyé Àgbò,
Oun ti bí erin àti ẹfọ̀n
Ó sì bí Àgbò ṣe ẹ̀kẹta.
Nígbàtí Ṣàngó bú mọ́ erin àti ẹfọ̀n,
Wọ́n bé lu igbó.
Ṣùgbọ́n Ṣàngó bú mọ́ Àgbò,
Àgbò náà sì bú mọ́ òun.
Òun kò sálọ; òun jà pẹ̀lú Ṣàngó.
Nígbàtí ó pẹ́ tí wọ́n ti ńjà, Ṣàngó fàsẹ́hìn
ó padà sí ọ̀run
Láti ìgbànáà Ṣàngó ti wà l'ọ́run.
Àti nígbàtí àpáàrá bá sán, ti mọ̀nàmọ́ná kọ,
Àgbò á fi ẹsẹ̀ wa ilẹ̀ á ní:
Ìjà òun pẹ̀lù rẹ̀ tún ku ẹ́kan.

8:2

ÀSỌYÉ

This is a teaching on courage in the face of overwhelming odds and an ongoing commitment to constant struggle. It begins with a teaching on the nature of things and within it, a rightful sense of expected regularity. That is to say, thunder comes in rainy season; there is no way to hide lightning as it flashes in the heavens and neither male or female partridges have identifying crests on their heads. This sets the context for the narrative on Agbo, the Ram, who reaches beyond the regular and the routine and achieves the unexpected and uncommon. Though smaller and less strong physically than the elephant or buffalo, in the end, he exhibits more courage and determination than either of them. Moreover, Agbo, the Ram, is singled out as the third child to distinguish him from the favored first-born. On still another level, one would not expect this from him. But he is the first-born of courage, determination and commitment, one who would not run, who roars at one who roars at him, who wrestles with the spirit of thunder, and who always stands ready for the ongoing struggle. He breaks the mould; he thunders at thunder and wears an invisible crest and crown on his head. Thus, the light of his deeds does not flash in secret but streaks across the heavens like lightning and is known world-wide.

9

9:1

The powerful person craves the crown.
This was the teaching of Ifa for Ogun.
He was advised to sacrifice.
The symbols of the sacrifice:
a sword, a rooster and a roasted yam.
Ifa said that it was the sword which Ogun would use in the pursuit of prosperity.
And that he should carry it with him everywhere.
Ogun was advised to eat the roasted yam and he ate it.
When he became thirsty, he went to the river to drink some water.
When he had finished drinking the water, he saw two people quarelling over a fish they had caught
Ogun told them that they should be patient
And that they should divide the fish and go home.

9:1

But they refused.
The first person said he came from the West.
The second person said she came from the East.
After hearing what they both had to say
concerning the matter,
Ogun took the sword which he had in his hand
and cut the fish into two equal parts
for them.
The first person thanked him and said that he
wanted him to open a way for him
so that he might reach his city.
He said that Ogun would become a prosperous
person.
He said that he would acquire an abundance of
good things.
And that he would suffer no hardship before
before reaching his city.

9:1

The second person also thanked Ogun
And she asked that Ogun not neglect to open the way for her to her city in the same way.
Ogun told them that he understood.
Therefore, since the day that Ogun divided the fish into two for the two people who were quarrelling
He has been called Ògúndáméjì, Ogun who divides into two equal parts.

ÒGÚNDÁ MÉJÌ
9

9:1

Alágbára ni ńsọkún adé li.
A dífá f'Ògún.
A níkí ó rúbọ.
Ẹbọ: àgada, àkúkọ àti iṣu sísun.
Ifá ní: àgada yẹn ni Ògún màá fiṣe iṣẹ́ ọrọ̀
Kí ó màa múu l'ọ́wọ́ káàkiri.
A níkí kí ó jẹ iṣu sísun. Ó jẹẹ́.
Òrùngbẹ sì ńgbẹẹ́, ó lọ sí odò lọ mu omi.
Bí ó ti mu omi tán, ó rí àwọn méjì tí ńjà
nítorí ẹja kan tí wọ́n pa.
Ògún níkí àwọn méjì náà mú sùúrù
Kí wọ́n lọ pín ẹja náà lọ n'ilé ṣùgbón wọ́n kọ̀
Èkìíní ṣo pé ìwọ̀-oòrùn ni òun ti wá.
Èkejì sì ṣo pé ìlà-oòrùn ni òun ti wá.
Lẹ́hìn gbogbo eyítí wọ́n ṣo fún un,
Ògún fi àdá tí ó wà ni ọwọ́ rẹ̀ dá ẹja náà si
méjì fún àwọn

9: 1

Ekìíní dúpé l'ọwọ́ rè ó ní òun fẹ́ kí ó là
ọ̀nà wá dé ìlú òun.
Ó ní Ògún á ṣodi ọlọ́rọ̀
Ó ní ọwọ́ rẹ̀ yóo tẹ̀ ọ̀pọlọ́pọ̀ nkan
Ti ojú kò niifi pọ́n ọn kí ó tó dé ọ̀dọ̀ oun.
Ẹnikejì tún dúpé, ó bẹ̀ kí Ògún má sài là ọ̀nà
wá dé ìlú òun bákan náà.
Ògún ní òuń gbọ́
Njé ọjọ́ ti Ògún ti dá ẹja si méjì fún àwọn méjì
tí ńjà
Ni a ti ńpe ní Ògúndáméjì.

ÒGÚNDÁ MÉJÌ
9

9:1

ÀSỌYÉ

This is a teaching on the right use of power as a means to open the way for oneself by opening the way for others. It begins with the assertion that a powerful person usually seeks ultimate or maximum power which is symbolized here by the "craving for the crown," i.e., the power of the royal ruler and all its benefits. The text says literally "the powerful person cries for the crown--*sọkún adé*." Given such a craving for maximum power, the person of power must sacrifice in order to use power rightfully and to cultivate moderation in one's desire for increase in power. It suggests that we don't all have to be kings and queens to live a good life and that serving, itself, is greatly rewarding. This Odu offers three objects of sacrifice which at the same time are symbols of areas of self-sacrifice. (A similar symbolic offering is recommended in Odu 119:2 to teach on the need and value of work.)

Here the prescribed sacrifice for the person is the sword, the rooster and the roasted yam. The sword is to be sacrificed as a weapon of war and aggression and used instead to "open the way--*là ọnà*," to the good life. The rooster is to be sacrificed as a giving up of the aggressive arrogance of power, in a word, the "cockiness" associated with the rooster or cock. And the roasted yam serves as a symbol of the sacrifice of physical needs and comfort whose pursuit with power could lead to excesses against others and destructive self-indulgence.

Ogun is the perfect example and focus for this narrative on power, for he is the orisha of war, iron, technology and related areas. He is told at the outset that his sword will be the key instrument in his pursuit of prosperity, or the good life. It is both the symbol and source of his power, the instrument of his work and the opener of his way to the good life. When he sees the two people fighting over a fish they both have caught, he could have simply took the fish for himself through killing them, robbing them or both. Instead, he acts as judge and advises patience and the sharing of a common good. When they refuse, he uses his sword, his power, to cut the fish in two.

By this act, he "opens the way" for their sharing and thus the practice of justice. Justice here is a shared good and it reminds one of the ancient African teaching in the *Husia* of ancient Egypt in which the officials say, "I judged so that both parties were satisfied." It is important to note also that Ogun listens to each person before deciding and taking action. As judge, justice requires him to listen before deciding or acting, even though he had the power to impose his wishes arbitrarily. However, this would not have been justice but rather the arrogance or "cockiness" of power. As judge, his responsibility is to "open a way" for justice to emerge, a justice of shared good, regardless of whether one comes from the east or the west. And this is what he does.

In addition to using his power to open the way for justice, Ogun also uses his power to open a way for the traveller. This "way opening" is both literal and figurative, both actual and symbolic. He actually clears a road so that the two persons can use it to reach their respective cities--in the east and in the west. It is here that he is promised compensation for his work which points towards his realization of prosperity in abundance. The central lesson here is that it is by opening the way to good for others that we open the way to good for ourselves. The journey to the city is a metaphor for our journey through life to a good end. And Ogun's example of opening the way for himself, by opening the way for others is an invaluable model of how we can live full, good and meaningful lives.

ỌSÁ MÉJÌ
10

10:1

The head of a person with a bad future
does not swell up.
No one can recognize the footprints of a
madman on the road.
And, no one can distinguish the head of an
honorable person in an assembly of
people.
This was the teaching of Ifa for Mobowu,
Who was the wife of Ogun.
Surely, the head that will wear the crown
tomorrow,
No one can recognize it.
Therefore, let husband and wife stop calling
each other names,
And stop talking foolishly to each other.
For the head that will wear the crown
tomorrow,
No one can tell which one it will be.

10:1

Orí burúkú kìí wú tuulu.
A kì í dá ẹsẹ̀ aṣiwèrè mọ̀ lójú-ọ̀nà.
A kì í m'orí olóyè láwùjọ.
A dífá fún Móbówú
Tí í ṣe obìnrin Ògún
Orí tí ó jọba lọ́la,
Ẹnìkan ò mọ̀.
Kí tọkọ-taya ó mọ́ pe' ra.
Wọn ní wèrè mó.
Orí tí ó jọba lọ́la,
Ẹnìkan ò mọ̀.

10:1

ÀSỌYÉ

This is a teaching on the need for respect for everyone regardless of appearance or status. The sense given here is that we cannot always distinguish the person with a good or bad future, the sane or insane or the honorable and dishonorable nor the one who will become the royal ruler. And thus, we should be careful not to misjudge the value or importance of the person. On first reading, this may seem to be simple prudence to avoid offending one who might one day be in a position of power and thus, bring injury or loss to those who did not respect him or her. But at a deeper level, the Ifa tradition assumes an equal and inherent worthiness of all and here warns against failing to give each proper respect, regardless of appearance or current status.

Moreover, the metaphor of the possibility of any head becoming the one that wears the crown in the future speaks to the assumption of human potentiality. Here we read the "crowned head" as the one who flourishes. And we respect others not only because we recognize their inherent worth, but also because not respecting them could diminish their human potential, destroy a potential genius and deprive a head a crown of achievement that would have been its destiny and rightful heritage. Such a blocking and preventing of human development is clearly immoral and therefore this text suggests we should not distinguish persons in ways that diminish their dignity or fail to take into account the human potential inherent in each of us.

10:2

This is the teaching of Ifa for Odu,
Obarisa and Ogun,
When they were coming from heaven to earth.
Odu asked: "O Olodumare, *Lord of Heaven*,
this earth where we are going,
What will happen when we arrive there?"
Olodumare said that they were going to make
the world
So that the world will be good.
He also said that everything that they were
going to do there,
He would give them the *aṣẹ*, power and authority,
to accomplish it,
So that it would be done well.

Odu said "O Olodumare this earth where
we are going,
Ogun has the power to wage war.

10:2

And Obarisa has the aṣẹ to do anything
he wishes to do.
What is my power?
Olodumare said: "you will be their mother forever.
And you will also sustain the world."
Olodumare, then, gave her the power.
And when he gave her power, he gave her
the *spirit* power of the bird.

It was then that he gave women the power
and authority so that anything men
wished to do,
They could not dare to do it successfully
without women.
Odu said that everything that people would
want to do,
If they do not include women,
It will not be possible.

10:2

Obarisa said that people should always respect
women greatly.
For if they always respect women greatly, the world
will be in right order.

Pay hommage; give respect to women.
Indeed, it is woman who brought us into being
Before we became recognized as human beings.
The wisdom of the world belongs to women.
Give respect to women then.
Indeed, it was a woman who brought
us into being.
Before we became recognized as human beings.

10:2

A dífá fún Odù, Òbàrìṣà àti Ógún
Nijọ́ tí àwọ̀n ńti'kọle ọ̀run bọ̀ wá ilé ayé.
Odù ní: Ìwọ Olódùmarè; ó ní, ilé ayé
l'àwọn ńlọ yìí,
Ó ní, nígbàtí àwọn bá dé ọ̀hún nkọ́?
Olódùmarè ní kí wọ́n ó lọ máa ṣe ilé ayé kí ilé
ayé ó dára.
Ó ní gbogbo ohun tí wọ́n yìó bá sì máa,
Ó ní òun ó fún wọn l'aṣẹ ti wọ́n ó máa fi ṣee,
Ti yìó sì fi máa dára.

Odù ní: Ìwọ Olódùmarè; ilé ayé t'àwọn ńlọ yìí,
Ògún l'ágbára ogun jíja.
Ó ní: Òbàrìṣà, òun náà l'aṣẹ làti ìṣe gbogbo
ohun t'ó bá fẹ́ ṣe.
Ó ní kíni agbára ti òun?
Olódùmarè ní "ìwọ l'ó máa jẹ́ iyá wọn lọ láìláí.
Ó ní ìwọ ni o ó sì mú ilé ayé ró."
Olódùmarè l'ó bá fún òun l'ágbára.
Nígbàtí ó fún òun l'ágbára, ó fún òun l'ágbára ẹyẹ.

10:2

Ni ó gbé fún obìnrin l'aṣẹ wípé gbogbo
ohun yìó wù,
Okùnrin kò gbọ́dọ̀ lè dá nkankan ṣe l'ẹ́hìn obìnrin.
Odù ní gbogbo ohun tí ènìyàn bá ńṣe,
Ti kò bá fi ti obìnrin kún un,
Ó ní kò lè ṣe ṣe.
Òbàrìṣà ní kí wọ́n ó máa fi ìbà fún obìnrin
Ó ní ti wọ́n bá ti ńfi ìbà fún obìnrin,
Ilé ayé yìó máa tòrò.

Ẹ kúnlẹ̀' o; ẹ kúnlẹ̀ f'óbìnrin, o.
Obìnrin l'ó bí wa
K'áwa tó d'ènìyàn.
Ọgbọ́n ayé t'óbìnrin ni.
Ẹ kúnlẹ̀ f'óbìnrin.
Obìnrin l'ó bí wa
K'áwa tó d'ènìyàn.

10:2

ÀSỌYÉ

This is a teaching on the cooperative creation of the world. It, like Odu 248:1, provides a critical segment of the creation narrative, explaining the order of things at the beginning and the establishment of the principle of male/female equality in the creation, structuring and functioning of the world and in all things of importance. The Odu opens with Olodumare, Lord of Heaven and the source of all beings, sending three divine beings to complete the work of creation. Up to this point, as other texts tell us, the world is only a watery and marshy possibility. Olodumare thus sends the divine ones *to make the world good* and gives them the ase so that they could do their work well. The word used here is "*dara*" which means *good,* not only in the sense of beneficial and suitable to a purpose, but also pleasant and enjoyable. Here we have the affirmation of the *inherent goodness* of the world, an inherent goodness God ordains at the beginning of creation.

Secondly, we are instructed that the divine beings represent male and female principles in and of the world, each with an equal yet different power and authority, i.e., *aṣẹ*, to be used to complete creation cooperatively. Special attention, however, is given to defining the role of the female principle or woman in the world. Two major roles are assigned to woman -- *mother of the world* and *sustainer of the world*. To be mother of the world clearly speaks to a joint effort with the father of the world to reproduce and insure continuity and to nurture, care for and teach. But to be sustainer of the world is a wider role and one rich in possibilities of performance. However, we know from other texts that this role is above all related to the role of creator and guardian of culture, learning, refinement and flourishing of humanity and the world which includes a vast field of social responsibility which ranges from rulership to education. This is reaffirmed by the fact that in Odu 248:1 it is Oshun, the embodiment of culture, learning and human flourishing, who accompanies the male divine powers to make the world good.

The Odu next turns to a teaching on the special respect we should have for women as partners who are indispensable to the success of anything that men attempt to do and to the right order in and of the world. Finally, the Odu stresses the special respect we should all hold for women as women. In a sense, it is reaffirmation of the need for respect for women as both mother and sustainer, not only in the larger world sense, but especially in the personal and deeply human sense of bringing us in the physical and social, i.e., cultural being.

Again in the best of Ifa tradition and African tradition in general, all humans, men and women, have equal inherent worthiness or dignity. But here the text asks us to give added respect to women, for their role in bringing us into being before we become recognized as human beings. The text literally says "before we become human beings." But the extended sense suggests the reading as "before we become *recognized* as human beings." This period of not being recognized as human being seems to refer to the period in Yoruba and other African societies before the baby has been incorporated into society. It is the time when the baby has no name and is only a potential person. After seven or eight days, when the child appears to be a permanent member of the family, s/he is given a name and status and thus, is "recognized as a human being," not a spirit or *àbíkú*, i.e., one reluctant to live in the material world.

In this period of transition and possibility, it is our mothers who not only bring us into being physically, but begin the process of cultural nurturing which lays the basis for our social incorporation. In a word, she molds us in the image and interest of human society. And it is for her giving us this physical and cultural birth that the text tells us we should respect her in a special and meaningful way.

In addition, the text tells us we should respect women as the possessors of wisdom in the world. This, in the Ifa theological narrative, refers to the special power of knowledge and spirit power symbolized by the bird given to women by the Lord of Heaven, Olodumare, at the beginning of the creation. In *Kawaida* tradition, this text reaffirms the need to respect women as rational and knowledgeable human beings as well as actual or potential mothers and sustainers of the world. Thus, the moral obligation here is to respect women in their wholeness and as indispensable in bringing into being, physically and culturally, the human person. And it also reaffirms the equality and indispensability of women in the structure and functioning of the world and the ongoing requirement of male and female cooperation in any project of importance.

10:3

Ah, an elder who commits excess will be
thoroughly disgraced.
This was the teaching of Ifa for Odu
When Odu arrived on earth.
Ah, they said, "O you, Odu;"
They said "you must be careful.
You must be patient.
And you must not be shamelessly
disrespectful."
Odu asked "why?"
They said "it is because of the power
Which Oludumare has given you."

10:3

Há! Àgbà tí ó bá ṣe àṣejú títé níí tẹ́.
A dífá fún Òdù
Nígbàtí Òdú délé ayé.
Há! Wọ́n ní "ìwo, Òdú."
Wọ́n ní "ò bá ṣọ́ra rẹ.
Kí o sì ṣe sùúrù.
Kí o má yààjú."
Òdù ní "èétirí?"
Wọ́n ní nítorí agbára rẹ̀
Tí Olódùmarè fún un.

10:3

ÀSỌYÉ

This is a teaching on how one who is an elder and powerful person should act, especially toward others. It begins by asserting that an elder will lose respect if she commits excesses. The moral prohibition against excess (*àṣejù*) indicates both an ethical concern with balance and propriety. In the first case, balance is prescribed as a central virtue in Ifa tradition and appears as an emphasis throughout the Odu. A balanced person becomes a model of the moral person, one who has no habits or tendencies which lead to disgrace, self-destruction or self-diminishing.

Propriety, as a moral category, suggests the rightness of doing what is fitting, appropriate and in conformity with accepted moral and social standards. An elder should be concerned with the dignity and respect required of one holding such a status. And a powerful person must likewise act in such a way that s/he is not abusive or a disgrace to her/his office. Odu, as a powerful elder, is advised to be careful and patient and not to be shamefully disrespectful. Here careful refers to maintaining a considerateness towards others which is respectful and caring. The virtue of patience is a central Ifaic virtue and complements the virtues of calmness and self-control, so essential to good character, *ìwàrere*.

10:4

The hand of a child cannot reach the
high shelf.
And the hand of the elder is too large
to enter the mouth of the gourd.
The work the child humbly asks an
elder to do,
The elder should not refuse to do.
All of us have work to do for each
other's good.

Ọwọ́ èwe ò tó pẹpẹ,
Ti àgbàlagbà ò wọ akèrègbe.
Isẹ́ èwe bẹ àgbà.
Kí ó má ṣe kọ̀ mọ́.
Gbogbo wa la níṣẹ́ a jọ ńbẹ'ra wa.

10:5

Osa, the brightly shining one, Babalawo
of the world,
Interpreted the teachings of Ifa for the earth.
They said that the earth should stop making
sacrifices for wealth,
And instead make sacrifices that would
protect earth from its enemies.
In this way, we will live.
And so we plead
That as long as we live on earth,
That the earth not be destroyed.

Ọsá yòóò, babaláwo ayé,
Ló dífá f'áyé.
Wọ́n láyé ó f'ẹbọ ọlá lẹ̀
Ẹbọ ajogun ní ó ṣe.
Ǹjẹ́ àwa ńbẹ̀,
À ńbẹ̀
Àwa mọ̀ọ́ mọ̀ ńbẹ l'áyé o,
Ayé ò níí parun.

Ọ̀SÁ MÉJÌ
10

10:6

If all people were destined to be buried in
coffins,
All the iroko trees in the forest would have
been used up.
This was the teaching of Ifa for Owere, one
called struggle,
Who was coming from heaven to earth.
They said we are constantly struggling, all of us.
We are constantly struggling.
Those who choose good destinies are not many.
Thus, we are continuously struggling, all of us.
We are continuously struggling.

10:6

Bí ó bá ṣe pé gbogbo orí gbogbo ní í sun pósí,
Ìrókò gbogbo ìbá ti tán n'ígbó.
A dífá fún Òwèrè,
Tí ńtí Ìkọ̀lé ọ̀run bọ̀ wá sí t'ayé.
Wọ́n ni ówèrè là ńjà, gbogbo wa.
Òwèrè là ńjà,
Ẹni tó yan'rí rere kò wọ́pọ̀ .
Òwèrè là ńjà, gbogbo wa.
Òwèrè là ńjà.

ÌKÁ MÉJÌ

I I

I I : I

Ibarere, one who pays hommage from afar,
the priest of fire,
Interpreted the teachings of Ifa for fire.
They said that wherever fire emerges,
It will make a way for itself.
They said its head will clear a way for it.
Ifa says that anyone who wants to achieve
anything,
That person should practice sacrifice
So that a way can be opened for him,
As it is opened for fire.
For if a person practices sacrifice,
Anything she wishes to accomplish,
Whether it is work or some other
important thing,
That thing can be done.

ÌKÁ MÉJÌ

I I

I I : I

Ibarere, awo iná,
A dífá fún iná.
Wọ́n ní ibikíbi tí iná fi orí lé,
Ni yió jẹ́ ọ̀nà fún un.
Wọ́n ni orí rẹ̀ yió la ọ̀nà fún un.
Ifá ní ẹnìkan ńfẹ́ ṣe ohun kan,
Kí olúwarẹ̀ bá rúbọ,
Kí ọ̀nà ba lè là fún un,
Bí ó ṣe là fún iná.
Nítorítí bí olúwarẹ̀ bá rúbọ,
Ohunkóhun tí ó fẹ́ ṣe,
Ìbáṣe iṣẹ́ ni tàbí bí ó bá fẹ́ ṣe ohun
míràn pàtàkì,
Ohun náà yíò ṣe iṣẹ́.

ÒTÚRÚPỌ̀N MÉJÌ
12

12:1

Even a wise person cannot tie water into a
knot on the hem of a garment.
And no sage knows the number of grains of
sand on the ground.
The Ifa teachings were interpreted for Ori.
Ifa was also interpreted for character.
Ori asked the interpreters whether he could
have all the good things of life.
He was asked to practice sacrifice.
He practiced it.
And when he practiced sacrifice,
He had all the good things he wanted.

ÒTÚRÚPỌ̀N MÉJÌ
12

12:1

Olọ́gbọ́n kan ò ta kókó omi sétí aṣọ.
Ọ̀mọ̀ràn kan ó mọye èèpẹ̀ 'lẹ̀.
A dífá fórí.
A bù fún wà.
Orí ní ire gbogbo lè tó òun lọ́wọ́ báyìí?
Wọ́n ní ó rúbọ.
Ó sì rú u.
Ìgbà tí ó rúbọ tán,
Ó sì ní gbogbo ire tí ó nfẹ́.

ÒTÚRÚPỌ̀N MÉJÌ
12

12:2

It is the Ethiopian sparrow which builds
its own nest,
And puts its entrance face down in a curve.
The nest neither touches the water nor touches
the sky,
But its entrance points down in a curve.
This was the teaching of Ifa for Oyeepolu
Offspring of those who perform the ancestral
rites of Ife,
One whose mother left him all alone when he
was very young.
Thus, when Oyeepolu grew up,
He did not know all the rites of his ancestors.
His life became chaotic.
He sought a wife to marry but could not
find one.
And he did not have even a place he could
call home.

12:2

Then, he took his situation under consideration
And went to a babalawo for advice.
He was advised that it was because of his
ancestral rites
Which he had neglected
That he was in such confusion.
He was told to go to the graves of his ancestors
And to pay hommage and ask guidance.
After he had done so,
He started to enjoy his life.

12:2

Alapàndèdè l'ó kọ́lé tán,
L'ó kọjú rẹ̀ sódòòdo.
Kò kànmi, kò kànkè;
Ó wá kọjú re sódòòdo.
A dífá fún Oyèépolú,
Ọmọ ìṣòrò n'Ífẹ̀,
Èyítí ìyá rẹ̀ ó fi sílẹ̀
Ní òun nìkan ṣọṣọ léńje léńje.
Ìgbàtí Oyèépolú dàgbà tán,
Kò mọ ohun orò ilé baba rẹ̀ mọ́.
Gbogbo nǹkan rẹ̀ wá dàrú.
Ó wá obìnrin, kò rí.
Bẹ́ẹ̀ ni kò rí ilé gbé.
L'ó bá méjì kẹ́ta,
Ó lọ oko aláwo.
Wọ́n ní gbogbo nńkan orò ilé baba rẹ̀
Tó ti gbàgbé,
L'o ń'dà a láàmú.
Wọ́n ní kí ó lọ sí ojú oórì àwọn baba rẹ̀
Kí ó máa lọ júbà
Ìgbà tí ó ṣe bẹ́ẹ̀ tán
L'ó wá bẹ̀rẹ̀ síí gbádùn ara rẹ̀.

Òtúrá Méjì

13

13:1

Lying does not mean that one will not
become rich.
And breaking commitments does not
mean that one will not reach
an old age.
But on the day of death, the sacrifice
will be required.

Irọ́ pípa kìí wípé k'á má lówó.
Ilẹ̀ dídà kìí wípé k'á má dágbá.
Ṣùgbọ́n ọjọ àti sùn l' ẹbọ.

ÒTÚRÁ MÉJÌ
13

13:1

ÀSỌYÉ

This is a teaching on the possibility of wrongdoing gaining advantage in this life and the certainty of its disadvantage in the next life. It concedes that wickedness may gain wealth and that betrayal or breaking commitment does not prevent one from reaching old age. But it also expresses the profound conviction central to Odu ethics, that in the end one will have to answer for the wrong one does. This reflects the Yoruba belief in divine judgment and in the eventual triumph of right whether in this life or the next. It recalls and parallels the ancient Egyptian Husitic teaching that those who violate the laws of Maat (rightness) are eventually punished whether in this life or the next. The *Book of Ptahhotep* says "although wickedness may gain wealth, wrongdoing has never brought its wares to a safe port. In the end, it is Maat that endures and enables a person to say `it is the legacy of my father and mother'." Thus, in both texts, gains from wrongdoing are not enduring gains. On the contrary, the texts suggest rightness is the real and lasting achievement and reward in this life and the next.

13:2

The unrestrained mouth;
The mouth that cannot govern itself.
The trap set by the mouth never fails to
catch victims.
It is the mouth of the talkative which causes
the talkative to suffer.
It is the mouth of one who talks overmuch
which brings suffering to him.
It is the mouth which talks too much that
causes one suffering who talks
excessively.
What the eye sees,
The mouth talks about.
When the mouth talks,
It is torn apart like a piece of cloth.

13:2

Àyóóró ẹnu.
Àyòòrò ẹnu.
Èbìtí ẹnu ò tàsé.
Ẹnu ofóró níí pofóró.
Ẹnu ofòrò níí pofòrò.
Ẹnu fórofòro níí pòfóró.
Bí ojú bá rí,
Ẹnu a wí.
Bí ẹnú bá wí,
Ẹnu a sì ya pààrà paara bí aṣọ.

14:1

The teachings of Ifa were interpreted for
Aduke, she who everyone indulges,
An offspring of the kind-hearted people
of ancient times,
Who cooked a simple dish of maize and beans
so that they might acquire character.
She woke up early in the morning,
Weeping and chanting the funeral song of
sorrow for the loss of good in her life.
Aduke was advised to sacrifice.
And she did so.
After she had practiced sacrifice.
She gained honor.
She acquired wealth.
And all the good she was looking for,
She was able to grasp it firmly in her hands.

ÌRẸTẸ̀ MÉJÌ

14

14:1

A dífá fún Ádùkẹ́,
Ọmọ olóore àtijọ́tijọ́,
Asẹ̀wà ọ̀sọ̀sọ̀ ríwà.
Ó jí ní kùtù,
Ó nfomi ojúú ṣògbérè ire.
Wọ́n ní kí Ádùkẹ́ ó rúbọ.
Ó sì ṣe bẹ́ẹ̀.
Ìgbà tí ó rúbọ tán,
Ó sì l'ọ́lá.
Ó lówó lọ́wọ́.
Gbogbo ire tí ó ńwá pátápátá
Ni ó tẹ̀ ẹ́ lọ́wọ́.

14:2

The fine sand which children play with on
the road to the land of Ilesa,
If it is used to teach children how to walk,
It can also be used to teach them how to
walk gracefully.

Bùtùbútú ọ̀nà Ìjèsà lọmọdé fií ṣeré,
Bí ó bá kọ́mo ní rírìn ẹsẹ̀
A kọmọ ní yíyan.

15:2

The torrent breaks through hills and valleys.
This was the teaching of Ifa for Orunmila.
Who would triumph on earth,
And would do likewise in heaven.
Orunmila was told to sacrifice.
He was told he would triumph over his enemies.
And indeed when he practiced sacrifice,
He was victorious.

Àgbàrá làkè, lalẹ̀.
A dífá fún Ọ̀rúnmìlà
Yóò ṣẹ́gun ayé;
Yóò sì ṣẹ́ tọ̀run.
Wọ́n ní kí Ọ̀rúnmìlà rúbọ.
Wọ́n ní yóò ṣẹ́gun ọ̀tá rẹ̀.
Ìgbàtí ó rúbọ tán,
Ó sì ní ìṣẹ́gun.

ÒFÚN MÉJÌ

16

16:1

The soles of the feet are always flat.
The teachings of Ifa were interpreted for
the one who cannot be conquered.
One who cannot be conquered is another
name for mountain.
Many years from today,
The mountain will be as alive and firmly
established as ever.
The mountain is always as firmly established
as ever.
The mountain, the mountain, firmly established.
Years and years from now,
The mountain will remain immortal and
immovable.
Immovable is the mountain,
The mountain which is firmly established.

Òfún Méjì

16

16:1

Àtẹ́lẹsẹ̀ abara pẹ́lẹ́bẹ́.
A dífá fún ẹni-apáòká.
Ẹni-apáòká lorúko à á pòké.
Ọgún ọdún òní o,
Òkè ńbẹ láìkú gbọingbọin.
Gbọingbọin mọ̀ ni tòkè,
Òkè, òkè gbọingbọin.
Ọgbọ̀n ọdún òní o,
Òkè ńbẹ láìkú gbọingbọin.
Gbọingbọin ni tòkè,
Òkè, òkè gbọingbọin.

16:2

Rumor mongering destroys servants.
Breaking commitments destroys friends.
And damnation destroys thieves.
If a market closes down suddenly,
The crowd will be left scattered here and there.
But the real buyers will remain.
As will the traders who have spread their
goods for sale.

Àfíntí ni p'ọmọọ̀dọ̀
Ilẹ̀ dídà ni p'ọ̀rẹ́
Èpè ní p'olè
Bọ́jà bá tú pẹ́
Á ku èrò kàtàkàtà
Á ku anájà
À ku apàte.

16:3

Ifa says that we should not break a commitment to a friend.
Lest we die an unexpected death.
If we discuss something with a person,
And that person wants to break a promise to us,
The ancestors will judge him.

Ifá ní kí á má dalẹ̀ ọ̀rẹ́.
Kí á má baà kú ìkú àìrò tẹ́lẹ̀.
Bí a bá eníkan pèro ọ̀rọ̀ kan,
Bi olúwarẹ̀ nfẹ̀ dalẹ s'ẹni,
Arà ọ̀run ni yíò ṣè dájọ́ ọ̀rọ rẹ̀.

OGBÈ'YẸ̀KÚ
17

17:1

Ifa says he sees someone who owns neither
a calabash nor plate.
Everyone including her own relatives says she
has a bad destiny
And is making fun of her.
Ifa says this person will become important
in the near future
And that she will overcome all obstacles.

Ifá ní òun rí ẹnìkan tí kò ní igbá tí
kò ní àwo,
Ti gbogbo ènìyàn àti àwọn ara ilé
rẹ̀ nwípé ni olórí búburú
Tí wọ́n sì ńfi ṣé ẹlẹ́yà.
Ifá ní olúwarẹ̀ yió di ènìyàn ńlá
l'ẹ̀hìn ọ̀la
Àti pé yió sì má ṣẹ́gun gbogbo ìdíwọ́.

17:2

Ifa says that there is someone who has a title
Who will be replaced in his position.
And a person who stays in the background
Will be chosen to succeed him.
Everyone will rub their hands together
in honor of him.
And they will recognize and respect him.
There is also a divinity that was once revered
by all the people of a house.
But they do not revere him anymore.
And the forest has overgrown his shrine.
We should renovate the shrine.
And we should tie young palms fronds at the
entrance to it.
The person in the background that young and
old people are sneering at
Will indeed become a public figure.

17:2

Ifá ní ẹnìkan ni ó wà l'órí oyè yìí.
Tí a yíò pa n'ípò dà.
Tí a yíò fi enití wà ní ìkọ̀kọ̀ dípò rẹ̀.
Ẹni ìkọ̀kọ̀ náà ni gbogbo ará-ayé yíò
má rawọ́ sí òun.
Tí wọ́n yíò sì má júbà fún un.
Òrìṣà kan sì ni yìí ti gbogbo ilé ti ńsìn.
Tí wọ́n kò sì sìn mọ́.
Igbó sì kún bò ojúbọ rẹ̀.
K'á tún sẹe;
K'á sì ta mọ̀rìwò sí ẹnú ọ̀nà rẹ̀.
Ẹni ìkọ̀kọ̀ ti t'ọmọde t'àgba ti ńfi ojú tíínrín rẹ̀,
Dandan yíò di ẹni gbangba.

17:3

One who does not want to walk around naked,
Will find a seller of cloth when the
market opens.
This was the teaching of Ifa for Olofa, "the
ruler of Ofa who sells a box of velvet,"
The offspring of one who coughs like the
trumpeting of an elephant,
Descendant of one who uses a large container
to measure out jewels for his beloved,
The child of one who enjoys life moist and
smooth like a person eating honey.
Olofa, "the ruler of Ofa who sells a box of
velvet" was an old man
Who owned neither calabash nor plate.
But he had a large piece of cloth put away.
He did not allow himself to use it.
But others borrowed it to dress up and go out.
Olofa prepared himself and went to the babalawo.

17:3

And he asked them what he could do so that he
might gain importance.
They said that he should practice sacrifice,
including giving up the large piece
of cloth.
He heard and sacrificed.
Not the next day nor the next month, but the
king of Ofa eventually died.
Then, the people of Ofa made Olofa king,
Expecting that it would not be long before
he passed away.
But after he had assumed the office,
Instead of dying, he became increasingly stronger.
The life of the people of Ofa likewise
became good.
It became soft and easy for them.
And then they no longer wanted him to die.

17:3

Ifa says the person in the background will come
to the forefront.
She will achieve an important position.
And she will remain in this position a long time
before her passing.

17:3

Orí tí kò bá ni rìn ìhòhò,
Yíò rí aláṣọ nígbàtí ọjà tó.
A dá fún Ọ̀lọ́fà-a-tà-àpótí-àrán,
Ọmọ awúkọ́ gbinrin bí erin fọn,
Ọmọ a fi ìkòkò wọn ìlẹkẹ̀ fún àyànfẹ́ rẹ̀,
Ọmọ a j'ayé gbedegbede bí ẹni ńlá oyin.
Ọ̀lọ́fà-a-tà-àpótí-àran jẹ́ arúgbó,
Kòsí ní igbá tàbí àwo.
Ṣùgbọ́n ó ní aṣọ ńlá kan nínú odídì
Tí òun pàápàá kò jẹ́ lò,
Ṣùgbọ́n àwọn ènìyàn ní má tọrọ rẹ̀ lọ sóde.
Ọ̀lọ́fà múra ó tọ àwọn babaláwo lọ.
Ó bèèrè pé báwo ni òun yíò ti ṣo ní láári.
Wọ́n níkí ó rúbọ ni ifi pẹ̀lú aṣọ nlá.
Ó gbó; o rúbọ.
Kò l'ọjọ́, kò l'oṣù ọba Ọ̀fà kú.
Àwọn ára Ọ̀fà mú Ọ̀lọ́fà wọn fi jọba
Ní ìrétí pé kò ní pẹ́ kí ó tó kú.
Ṣùgbọ́n nígbàtí ó dé orí oyè tán,

17:3

Kàkà tí ibá fi kú íṣe, ni ara rẹ̀ túbọ̀ ńle sí.
Ayé àwọn ara Ọ̀fà sì wà dùn.
Ó sì dè fún wọn l'ọ̀rùn.
Wọ́n kò sì tún fẹ́ pé kí ó kú mọ́.
Ífá ní ẹni ikọkọ kan yíò di ẹni igbangba,
Tí yíò sì dé ipò ńlá kan,
Tí yíò sì pẹ́ púpọ̀ nínú ipò náà kí ó tó kú.

17:3

ÀSỌYÉ

This is a teaching on striving and succeeding against all odds, and on the promise of those in the background moving to the forefront through sacrifice and struggle. The Odu begins with a proverbial teaching on how we will and should find a way to do things which are necessary. It also suggests that a person of character will demonstrate his or her worthiness and will eventually get his or her due. This is exemplified by Olofa who is an old man, poor and of minor importance, but eventually becomes king.

Olofa is called "ruler of Ofa," even though poor and without power, to indicate both possibilty and promise. An ethics of character assumes that possibility lies in living a rightful life and that the promise of real prosperity, well-being and achievement is tied to and dependent on living a good life, sacrifice and struggle. Now the sacrifice and struggle are key because as Odu 43:1 says, even if we are going to die, we must wage a life and death struggle.

Olofa is contrasted with his father who is defined as having been strong "trumpeting like an elephant, wealthy, measuring out jewels in a large container" and happy enjoying a life as smooth and sweet as honey. Olofa is an old man, less strong, poor without calabash or plate, having only a long piece of velvet cloth. Moreover, he is not happy and is searching for a way to end his condition of unimportance.

The priest tells him to sacrifice. This is both a call for self-sacrifice, i.e., sacrifice of things that make the self unable to realize its potential, and a call to sacrifice objects, especially this one piece of cloth Olofa has. To sacrifice it, to give it up when it is the only thing he has is truly a lesson in sacrifice of smaller and replaceable things for that which endures and is irreplaceable.

The people of Ofa choose Olofa as king expecting he will die soon. But he becomes increasingly stronger. And he improves the life of the people and turns their wish for him to pass to a prayer for him to endure. The lesson here of giving to the people reinforces the lesson earlier when Ofu does not use his own cloth but shares it with others.

The lesson in both cases is that what we give returns in abundance. As Odu 95:1 says, i.e., "one who gives one thousand will receive two thousand in return."

Ọ̀YẸ̀KÚ OGBÈ
18

18:1

The hunter opens his pouch and pulls
out poison.
Aronimoja, the healer, unties his bag and
takes out medicine.
And the farmer seeks very soft ground in
which to cultivate his yams.
This was the teaching of Ifa for Oluorogbo
Who was the messenger of the king of earth
And who pounded palm nuts for Olushonsho,
the messenger of the king of heaven.
They said that if it should happen that the
earth falls into disorder,
Then Oluorogbo should set the earth right again.
And if heaven were to experience disorder,
Then Olushonsho would set heaven
right again.

Ọ̀YẸ̀KÚ OGBÈ
18

18:1

Ọdẹ ṣ'ápò yọ'ró.
Arónimọja tú àpò yọ òògùn.
Àgbẹ̀ wá ibi rírọ̀rírọ̀ kọ iṣu sí.
A dá fùn Olúorogbo,
Tí íṣe ikọ̀ àjàláyé
A lú ikin fún Olúṣonṣo,
Tí íṣe ikọ̀ àjàlọ́run.
Wọ́n ní bí ó bá dá kí ayé bàjẹ́,
Olúorogbo á tún ayé ṣe.
Bí ó bá dá kí ọ̀run bàjẹ́,
Olúṣonṣo á tún ọ̀run ṣe.

18:1

ÀSỌYÉ

This is a teaching on seeing all things in their proper place. The hunter kills and thus, pulls out poison; the healer heals and thus, makes available medicine; the farmers who produce crops look for the best soil in which to sow their seeds. This anticipated order of things, this expected regularity is reflected also in the teaching that the messenger of the king of earth is to set things right on earth and the messenger of the king of heaven is to set things right in heaven. Kawaida reads this as an obligation for us who are on earth to set the earth right when it goes wrong, to constantly put forth right and bring good into the world as Odu 78 teaches us. For such responsibility for bringing good into the world is the fundamental mission and meaning of human life. This is at the same time a teaching for those who would be so concerned about the affairs of heaven they are negligent in the affairs of earth. The affairs of heaven and responsibility for it rightly belong to the heavenly hosts, spiritual aides to the Lord of Heaven. Our simple yet demanding task is to constantly bring good into the world and make the world a good place in which to live and flourish.

OGBÈ ÌWÒRÌ

19

19:1

The teachings of Ifa were interpreted
for Odogbo
When he was in the midst of much trouble.
They said that this was the year that he
would achieve wealth.
They said he should sacrifice.
He heard and he complied.
They said that when he had practiced sacrifice,
He should go and pay hommage to his mother.
They said it is at home that his good fortune
would be found.
And that he should not go anywhere else.
When Odogbo had offered sacrifice,
And had also paid hommage to his mother,
He stayed home for four days.
But he did not see anything whatsoever like
good fortune.
On the fifth day, he got ready and went to
the farm for wood.
He said he would not die of hunger.

Ogbè Ìwòrì

19

19:1

When he arrived at the farm, he cut quite
a bit of firewood.
He then began to carry back as large a load
as possible.
As he was returning carrying his load,
The spirit of his mother appeared in the
form of a bird
And she began to speak saying:
"Odogbo, throw away the wood.
The good fortune arrived at your house
while you were gone."
When Odogbo heard this, he said he would
carry the wood home anyway.
When he arrived home, he threw the bundle
of wood to the ground
And it broke through the ground to a pit of beads.
In this way money and wealth came to Odogbo.
And he became a rich man.

19

19:1

A dífá fún Odogbo
Ni ọjọ́ ti ó wà nínú oyikiti ìpọ́njú.
Wọ́n ní ni ọdún yìí ni ọrọ̀ rẹ̀ pé.
Wọ́n ní kí ó rúbọ.
Ó gbọ́ , Ó rúbọ.
Wọ́n ní bí ó bá rúbọ tán
Kí ó lọ bọ ìyá rẹ̀.
Wọ́n ní ilé ni ire rẹ̀ wà
Kò gbọ́dọ̀ lọ sí ibikíbi.
Nígbàtí Odogbo rúbọ tán,
Tí ó sì bọ ìyá rẹ̀.
Ó jókòó sí ilé títí di ọjọ́ ẹ̀kẹrin,
Ṣùgbọ́n kò rí ohunkóhun bí ire.
Nígbàtí ó di ọjọ́ ẹ̀karùún Odogbo
múra lọ sí oko igi.
Ó ní óun kò ni jẹ́kí ebi kí ó pa òun kú.
Nígbàtí ó dé oko ó ṣé igi dáradára
Ó sì rú ni àrù tó ẹrù.

Ogbè Ìwòrì

19

19:1

Bí ó ti gbérù tí ó ńbọ̀,
Ìyá rè di ẹyẹ.
Ó sì bẹ̀rẹ̀ sí wípé.
Odogbo dà 'gi nù.
Ire ti délé l'ẹ̀hìn rẹ̀.
Nígbàtí Odogbo gbọ́ ó ní òun yíò rù igi
yìí délé.
Bí ó ti délé ti ó fi ìdí igi sọ'lẹ̀.
Bẹ̀ẹ̀ni ó jìn sí'lẹ̀ akún.
Báyìí ni owó dé tí ọlá dé,
Tí ó sì di olọ́rọ̀.

19:1

ÀSỌYÉ

This is a teaching on the need for moral reasoning in the context of tradition. It is a rare verse in that even though Odogbo seems to disobey instructions of the babalawo, he is not punished nor does he lose the good fortune promised him as in most cases of failure to comply. He is told to sacrifice and he does, but he is told to stay home and he does not.

Two things should be noted here. First, he does sacrifice which is the critical aspect of this moral tradition. Thus, he has done the essential thing. And secondly, he does stay home until he is presented with the possibility of starvation. Then, he chooses to live, even if he does not obtain a great fortune. Now he does not clearly defy the instruction of Ifa. He simply reaches a point where he must make a choice about the greater good: a) follow instructions which unchanged could lead to death, or (b choose life by reasoning through the instructions and seeing that morality is not simply following rules but finding ways to maintain principle in the context of changing and often conflicting circumstances. Here the greater good is preservation of life and the sacrifice required is to pass up the promise of fortune for the maintenance of life. Also, by going to get the wood, he is not simply waiting for good to come to him. In fact, his going out to get wood to save his life is the very way by which he comes into a double good fortune. Also instructive is his not throwing the wood away in spite of ancestor advice given by the spirit of his mother. This also suggests that we should think things through, recognize that we might not always read or hear our ancestors correctly, and having thought about things deeply and soberly, make a decision based on the best of our moral values and thinking as persons and as a people.

Finally, there remains the lesson that it is "at home," within ourselves, and among our friends, family and people, that we will always find the good fortune we might often seek elsewhere. This is a reaffirmation of Odu 147's teaching that "the very thing we are looking for is near us." So was the message for Odogbo and each of us. For it was when he returned home that he found the good fortune for which he was searching.

19:2

Plucking the feathers of a living fowl ruins it.
Not plucking the feathers of the fowl
leaves it with its splendor.
This was the teaching of Ifa for Ebu-Eyin,
internal deterioration,
Who is the senior sibling of war.
They said the people should sacrifice,
But they turned a deaf ear to the wisdom
of making sacrifice.
They were not wise to do so.
They were not perceptive.
They did not know that
It is at home that the war is lost before even
reaching the battlefield.

19:2

Títu níí m'ádìẹ bàjẹ́.
Àìtú níí m'ádìẹ ṣe yẹ̀gbẹ̀yẹ̀gbẹ̀.
Dífá fún Ẹ̀bù-Ẹ̀yìn,
Tíí ṣe ẹ̀gbọ́n ogún.
Wọ́n níkí wọ́n rúbọ.
Wọ́n kọtí ọgbọ́n ìṣẹbọ.
Ǹjẹ́ wọn ò gbọ́n ṣee.
Wọ́n ò mọ̀ràn.
Wọ́n ò mọ̀ wípé
Nílé l'ogun ti bàjẹ́ kí wọ́n tó
r'íbi ogun.

19:3

Those who are in the habit of throwing water in the streets,
You should throw it cautiously,
So that you might not wet your own guest.
This was the teaching of Ifa for Orunmila
Who was going to take Olojo, *the expected guest*, as wife
Olojo had promised to come within nine days,
But Olojo actually arrived in five.

Domi, domi.
E fèsò domi.
Kí ẹ má domi s'ólojò lára.
Dífá fún Ọ̀rúnmìlà
Tí ó ńlọ gb'Ólojò n'íyàwò.
Ìsán l'Ólojò dá,
Àrún l'Ólojò dé.

19:4

Bad conduct is what is attributed to youth.
Bad character is what is attributed to elders.

Ìṣekúṣẹ l'èwe lè ṣe.
Ìwà ìhùkuhù ni ti àgbàlagbà.

19:5

An elder who sits down without leaning back
Has the appearance of a person standing up.
This was the teaching of Ifa for Olayilokun,
whose name means "wherever honor turns it finds fortune."
She said that her strength was not adequate for the world.
But they said her strength would be equal to her tasks in the world.
They said she should sacrifice.

Ajókòó kò f'ẹ̀hìn ti àgba
Bí ẹnití ó nàró nírí.
L'ó dífá fún "olá-yí-lù-okùn"
Ó ní ipá oun kò ni ká ayé.
Wọ́n ní ipá rẹ̀ yíò ká ayé.
Wọ́n ní kí ó rúbọ.

OGBÈ'DI

21

21:1

Ogbedi Perepere was the one who interpreted
the teachings of Ifa for Ori,
Who had kneeled down and chosen his destiny,
And whom detractors were preventing
from achieving it.
Ifa says he sees the evil wishers who do not
want us to succeed in what we are doing.
Ifa says he will join us in overcoming the
evil wishers.
He says we should sacrifice.
When Ori had done what was due in
practicing sacrifice,
All that he was doing fell into place and
straightened out.
And the way became clear.

21:1

Ogbè-di-pẹ́rẹpẹ̀rẹ l'ó dífá fún Orí
Tí ó kúnlẹ̀ tí ó yàn ìwà rẹ̀,
Tí elénìní kò jẹ́kí ó ṣee.
Ifá ńi: òun rí àwọn aláròmọ́ tí wọn kò fẹ́ kí
a ṣeun kan ẹni.
Ó ńi: k'á rúbọ.
Ífá ní òun yíò bá eni ṣẹ́gun aláràmọ́ náà.
Nígbàtí Orí tó rúbọ,
Ni ohun gbogbo tí ó ńṣe tó gún.
Tí ò sí ní ọ̀nà.

21:2

Quietly I go, smoothly I return."
This was the teaching of Ifa for Ariwowo,
the Hook, the Grasper,
When he was waging war against a tangled knot.
They said he would not return empty-handed.
They said he should sacrifice.
He made the sacrifice.
Since then Ariwowo, the Grasper, has not
been empty-handed,
Even if he reaches to the top of a mountain
to pull something down.
Ifa says we are stretching out our hands
toward something.
Ifa says we should sacrifice
So that we may not be unsuccessful in that
for which we reach,
Whether it is in the work we do or something
else.

21:2

"Jẹ mi lọ, ṣe mi bọ̀."
L'o d'Ífá Aríwọ̀wọ́
Ti ó ngbógun lọ si i-n'iti.
Wọ́n ní kò ni ṣánwọ bọ̀.
Wọ́n ní ó rúbọ.
Ó rúbọ.
Látígbà náà ni Aríwọ̀wọ́ kìí ti ṣánwo,
Bí ó bá nà sí ò kè fà ohunkóhun.
Ifá ní a nnàwọ́ sí ohun kan.
Ifá níkí a rúbọ,
K'á má bá pòfo nínú nnkan tí à ńnawó sí náà.
Ìbáṣe iṣẹ́ tàbí nǹkan míràn.

OGBÈ'ROSÙN
23

23:1

The teachings of Ifa were interpreted
for Nwonmile
Who would see his father in a vision.
He said "I see my father today,
father of the leopard.
Father, come from heaven and help me.
The father of a child should not fail to
help his child."
Ifa says someone has forgotten his father.
And that if he does not take care of his father,
He will not find anyone on earth to take
care of him.
Ifa says this person should sacrifice
So that the way may become clear for him
in his affairs.
Indeed, something belonging to this person
will be completely ruined,
If he does not care for his father,
Whether his father is in heaven or on earth.

Ogbè'Rosùn

23

23: 1

A dífá Ifá Nwọnmile
Tí ó ńlọ rí baba rẹ̀ ni ojú àlá.
Ó ní: mo rí baba mi l'oní, ìbà ẹkùn.
Baba tí òrun wá gbé mi.
Iba ọmọ kò ṣàì gbe ọmọ rẹ̀.
Ifá ní ẹníkan gbàgbé baba rẹ̀.
Tí kò bá tọ́jú baba rẹ̀,
Kò ní rí ẹni tọ́jú òun náà ni ayé.
Ífá ní ó rúbọ,
Kí ọ̀ràn rẹ̀ bá lè ní ọ̀nà.
Nńkan eléyìí yíò bàjẹ́ pátápátá,
Bí kò bá tọ́jú baba rẹ̀,
Yálà bí ó wà ni ọ̀run tàbí ní ayé.

23:2

The elephant makes a place tremble
by virtue of its power.
And an ant's size cannot be compared to
that of a buffalo.
Ayinka, the one praised everywhere,
babalawo of the world,
Was the one who interpreted the teachings
of Ifa for the world.
The world was advised to sacrifice
So that good things might be said about it.
Ayin, the praiser is praised everywhere.
The mouth with which you praise me,
May you not turn it around against me.
For the praised one should be praised
everywhere.

23:2

Erin níí fi ibi mímì sọlá.
Eerà ò ni jọ̀bọ̀ tó ẹfòn.
Àyìnkà awo ayé
L'ó dífá fún ayé.
Wọ́n ní káyé ó rúbọ
Kí wọ́n lè ma sọ̀rọ̀ rẹ̀ ní rere.
Àyìn kà làá yin ayìn.
Ẹnu tí ẹ mú yìn mí
Ẹ má mà padà.
Àyìn kà làá yìn ayìn.

OGBÈ'ROSÙN
23

23:3

If we would listen to the teachings of Ifa,
We would last like our ancestors lasted.
If we would follow the teachings of
Ope, *Orunmila,*
We would grow old like the ancient ones.

B'ó bá ṣe wípé ti Ífá l'a bá ńgbọ́,
À bá pé bí ara iwájú ti pẹ́.
B'ó bá ṣe wípé tí Ọ̀pẹ̀ l'a bá ń tọ̀ lẹ́hìn,
À bá dàgbà bí ara ìgbàhun-ìgbàhun.

23:4

The teachings of Ifa were interpreted
for Orunmila
When he was going on a spiritual mission
on the shore of the ocean,
When he was in the middle of the lagoon
At the home of the sixteen owners of
the market.
They said Baba Orunmila would never
return home.
But it came to pass that Baba Orunmila began
to cry out in a powerful way, turning
his cry into a shout
And he turned his lamentation into a song
of sorrow.

23:4

He called out saying: Agbe bird, carry me home,
O' Agbe.
We do not go on a journey so that we may not
return home.
So, Agbe bird, please carry me home.
Then, before long and in the not distant future,
Come and join us in a victory achieved
through sacrifice;
Victorious in struggle as we have come to be.

23:4

A dífá fún Ọ̀rúnmìlà
Ifá nsawo lọ sí àpá òkun
T'òun ìlà méjì ọ̀sà,
Nílé ọlọ́jà mẹ́rìndínlógún.
Wọ́n ní Baba ò nìí padà délé.
Baba wá m'ekún ṣ'ẹkún ìgbe.
Ó fi ìyèrè ṣe ìyèrè aro.
Ó ní: Agbe gbé mi délé o ò Agbe.
A kìí ràjò k'á má délé o.
Agbe gbé mi délé o.
Kò pẹ́ kò jìnnà
E wá bá ni bá àrúṣẹ́ ogun
Àjàṣẹ ogun l'á wá wà.

27:1

A hassock has a hard chest.
This was the teaching of Ifa for Olokunde
whose name means "one who has the
the strength to endure will arrive,"
When she was crying and praying for a child.
They said that she should sacrifice.
They said that if she did not sacrifice, she would
still bear children.
But so that her children might not become
enemies to each other, she should
practice sacrifice.

Tìmùtìmù bí àyà pì.
L'ó dífá fún Olókundé,
Níjọ́ tí ó ńfi ẹkún ojú ńṣe ìráhùn ọmọ.
Wọ́n ní kí ó rúbọ.
Wọ́n ní bí kò rubọ́ yíò bímọ,
Ṣùgbọ́n kí àwọn ọmọ rẹ̀ má ba máa bá
ara wọn ṣe ọ̀tá ni kí ó rúbọ.

27:2

Ogbe achieved amazing things,
But the critics remained.
Ifa accomplished everything successfully,
But the slanderers continued to exist.
This was the teaching of Ifa for Edu, *Orunmila*,
Offspring of one who brings forth one
extraordinary thing after another,
Offspring of one who produces wonders upon
wonders.
The wonderous things which Ifa brings forth
cannot be ruined.
They simply continue to multiply.
And the wonderful things Ifa says that I am
to accomplish
Cannot be destroyed either.

27:2

Ogbè gbaradá tań.
T'ẹlẹ́gàn l'ó kù.
Ifá ṣe ohun gbogbo tań.
Ó ku tí ẹlẹ́nu.
A dífá fún Èdú,
Ọmọ agbápà l'ápà,
Ọmọ agbé rekete l'orí rekete.
Àrà tí Ifá dá,
Kò leè bàjẹ́.
Pípele níí pele.
Àrà tí Ifá níkí ndá,
Kò níí parun.

Ogbè'Gúndá

31

31:1

An uncontrolled temper does not create anything for anyone.
Patience is the father of character.
A person who is patient will become the master of all things.
She will reach a ripe old age.
He will live a healthy life.
And she will enjoy life thoroughly
Like a person tasting honey.

Inúbíbí kò dá nǹkan fún ẹni.
Sùúrú ni baba ìwà.
Ẹnití ó ni sùúrú ohun gbogbo l'ó ní.
À j'àgbó
À j'àtọ́
À' j'ayé rìndìn-rìndìn
Bí ẹni ńlá oyin.

31:2

Night falls and we spread out our
sleeping mats.
Day breaks and we roll the mats up.
One who weaves cotton yarn must wind it
while walking back and forth.
And when a person dies, we dig into the ground,
Going much too far down in the mind
of the timid.
This was the teaching of Ifa for Orunmila
When he was going on a spiritual journey to
the town of Ika.

Alẹ́ lẹ́ àá tẹ́ ẹní.
Ojúmọ́ mọ́ àá ká ẹní.
Adàwú ni pooyì rẹrẹ kálẹ̀.
Òkú l'ó kú ni a gbẹ́ ilẹ̀
L'ó jìn gbùngbùn l'ójú ojo.
A dá fún Ọ̀rúnmìlà
Níjọ́ tí ó ńṣawo re òde Ika.

31:2

ÀṢOYÉ

This is a teaching on doing what is appropriate when it is appropriate. It suggests we not delay doing what is necessary, nor be afraid to do our duty in taxing times. Thus, it says we must sleep when it is time and wake up when it is time. We must walk in the world in the appropriate way in order to weave the fabric of life we want. And when it comes time to deal with crisis or danger, we must have the courage to do so regardless of the depth to which we must dig or the extent to which we must go to achieve our ends.

The teaching suggests that often people seek magic formulas to living a good life. But this verse suggests that it is doing the simple, appropriate and necessary things that grounds our life and lays the basis for our successful dealing with larger and more complex things. Therefore, if we want a healthy life we must not simply wait until we get word from a doctor, but must begin by doing the simple things: being moderate and selective in what we eat and drink, exercising regularly, avoiding unnecessary stress and strain and at the end of work well done, finding a cool and peaceful place to rest adequately and think deeply about the future and consequences of things as Odu 1:1 teaches us.

31:3

Character is all that is required.
Character is all that is required.
There is no destiny that needs to be called
unfortunate in Ife city,
Character is all that is required.

Ìwà nìkan l'ó ṣòro o.
Ìwà nìkan l'ó ṣòro o.
Orí kan kìí, burú l'otù Ifẹ̀,
Ìwà nìkan l'ó ṣòro o.

31:3

ÀSỌYÉ

This is a teaching on character as the central, if not sole, determinant of a person's destiny. It is an extraordinary assertion within Odu ethics for at least two reasons. First, the Odu also teach that destinies are chosen by persons as spirits before coming to the world and that these are essentially unalterable. But there are passages throughout the Odu which suggest a moral life can and will in fact determine one's destiny. This passage on character is such a passage. For it clearly states that no destiny is *ipso facto* or needs to be bad or unfortunate, *buru*. For character is all that is required for a good one.

This passage is also important in its stress on character as the essence of the moral personality. It suggests that the cultivation and possession of character is the essential moral task and the ground for a good life in this world and the next. This suggests that character subsumes and makes possible the fulfillment of all other moral obligations.

31:4

What we hear is the sound of things
done loudly.
We do not hear the sound of things
done gently.
We drag the one who does things loudly to
the back door of the house of the
unpretentious person.
Orunmila says he does things gently when
he gives someone his destiny.
Ifa says that we should not engage in fighting,
And that we should sacrifice
So that our relatives will not injure us in the
evil of fighting.

31:4

Pàràpàrà gbìì n'ílẹ̀ l'a gbọ́.
A kí igbọ́ pẹ̀lẹ́pẹ̀lẹ́ gbíí.
Ẹ̀hìn lẹ̀kun ilé awurẹtẹtẹ l'àá ti wọ́ pàràpàrà lọ.
Ọ̀rúnmìlà ní ó a ṣe pẹ̀lẹ́pẹ̀lẹ́ fi ìwà jìn ẹni.
Ifá níkí a má ṣe jà.
Kí ẹnìkan rúbọ
Kí araalé rẹ̀ má bá ṣee nìjàmbá ní ibi ìjà.

OGBÈ'SÁ
33

33:1

The liar dies and dies in a forest of fire.
The wicked dies and dies on a sun-scorched
savannah.
But the righteous dies and dies peacefully,
Leaning back against a water jar decorated
with jewels.
Orunmila, priest of the world, interpreted the
teachings of Ifa for the people of
the world,
When they were creating a world,
A world where there was no peace,
A world where there was no harmony.
They were advised to sacrifice.
But only the righteous remained to
practice sacrifice.

OGBÈ'SÁ
33

33:1

So, speak truth; do justice
Be kind and do not do evil.
Truth travels on a narrow path
But the wicked wander on a wide road.
Speak truth; do justice
Do justice and speak truth.
For one who is righteous is supported by
the Divine.

OGBÈ'SÁ

33

33:1

Purọ́-purọ́ kú, ó kú s'ígbo iná.
Ṣika-Ṣika kú, ó kú s'ọ́dan òòrùn.
Ṣòótọ́-ṣòótọ́ kú, ó kú gbẹdẹmukẹ,
Ó fẹ̀hìnti àmù ìlẹ̀ké.
Ọ̀rúnmìlà awo ayé dífá fún ọmo aráyé
Nígbàtí wọ́n ńṣe ayé,
Tí ayé kò rójú,
Tí ayé kò jọ.
Wọ́n níkí wọ́n rúbọ.
Olóòtọ́ nìkan ní ńbẹ̀ l'ẹ̀hìn tí ńṣẹbọ
Ǹjẹ́ s'òtító; ṣe òdodo.
Ṣoore; má ṣìka.
Òtító a bọ̀nà tóóró.
Òsìkà a bọ̀nà gbàràrà.
Sọ òtító; ṣe òdodo.
Ṣòdodo; sòtítọ́.
Ẹ́nití ṣòtítọ́ ni ìmólé ńgbè.

OGBÈ'SÁ
33

33:1

ÀSỌYÉ

This is a teaching on the need and value of righteousness in the world. The wrongdoer who lies and is cruel is portrayed as one who does not find cool relief, but rather searing heat signified by the "forest of fire" and the "sun-scorched savannah." These metaphors for heat and discomfort are contrasted with the metaphor of leaning against the jeweled water jar which signifies not only relaxation in wealth, but also a coolness or calmness suggested by the image of water.

The verse urges us to practice two of the cardinal virtues of Ifaic and Maatian ethics: truth and justice. And it assures us that the righteous who practice these will be favored by the Divine. The verse also encourages us to "be kind"and not be evil. This joining of kindness to the virtues of truthfulness and justice is key to the care and responsibility we must feel and exercise toward one another. For both truth and justice can be harsh. And it is with loving kindness that they are balanced and serve their essential function of bringing and supporting good in the world. It is through kindness that the moral excellence of *ìwàpẹ̀lẹ́*, gentle character, is grounded and flourishes.

33:2

The teachings of Ifa were interpreted for
Eni-aye-kan, "one whose turn it is
to take responsibility for the world,"
And the same was done for Sheerere, "one
who does it well."
Do it well; bear the responsibility well.
Those whose turn it is to take responsibility
for the world,
They should do good for the world.
When it becomes your turn to take responsibility
for the world,
You should do good for the world.
When it becomes my turn to take responsibility
for the world.
May I bear the burden well.
And may I do good for the world.

33:2

A dífá fún Ẹni-ayé-kan.
A bù Ṣée-rere.
Ṣée-rere; gbé ẹrù rere.
Ẹni-ayé-kan,
Ẹ s'ayé ire.
Bí ó jẹ́ ìwọ l'ayé kan,
Kí o ṣ'ayé ire o.
Bí ó jẹ́ èmi l'ayé kan,
Kí mo gbé ẹrù rere.
Kí mo ṣ'ayé ire.

33:3

Even if a babalawo is in great need,
A babalawo should not lie.
And even if a healer is in difficult
circumstances,
A healer should not be dishonest.
Indeed, no one should lie or be dishonest.
This was the interpretation of Ifa for Orunmila
When unknown persons were waging war
against him.
He was advised to sacrifice.
He heard and made the sacrifice.

33:3

Bí ojú bá ń pọ́n babálawo,
Kí babaláwo má purọ́.
Bí ojú bá ń pọ́n oníṣègùn
Kí oníṣègùn má ṣe parọ́.
Gidi, k'ẹ́ni má sèké tàbí ṣe parọ́.
Dífá fún Ọ̀rúnmìlà
Níjọ́ ẹni àìmọ̀ wá ńkó ogun jà òun.
Wọ́n níkí ó rúbọ.
Ó gbọ́; ó rúbọ.

OGBÈ'KÁ
35

35:1

I stood for a long time,
But I was unable to reach the ishin fruit.
I bent down for a long time,
And I still could not reach the ishin fruit.
But thanks to some special elders
Who advised me to prostrate myself in respect and without reservation,
I prostrated myself in respect and without reservation.
Then, the ishin fruit dropped into my hands.
And the ishin fruit dropped into my mouth.
This was the teaching of Ifa for Ejika-gogoogo
Who was going to carry Osu to the sacred grove of Ifa.
They were advised to sacrifice.
They heard and complied.
May Osu stand up straight.
May he not lie down.
Standing firm and upright is how we must
always find Osu.

35

35:1

Mo dúró-dúró,
Ọwọ́ mi ò tó iṣin.
Mo bẹ̀rẹ̀-bẹ̀rẹ̀,
Ọwọ mi ò tó iṣin.
Ọpẹ́lọpẹ àwọn àgbà kan,
Tí wọ́n níkí ndọ̀bálè yẹ́kẹ́.
Mo dọ̀bálè yẹ́kẹ́.
Isin ńbọ́ sí mi l'ọ́wọ́.
Isin ńbó sí mi l'ẹ́nú.
Dífá fún Èjíkà-gògòògò
Tí yíò gbé Òsù dé'gbódù.
Wọ́n ní kí wọ́n rúbọ.
Wọ́n gbọ́; wọn rú.
Ǹjẹ́ Òsù m'órí ró o.
Kí ó má dùbúlẹ̀.
Ìdúró gángán l'àá bá Òsù.

OGBÈ'KÁ
35

35:1

ÀSỌYÉ

This is a teaching on self-surrender and mastery of the teachings of Ifa as a foundation for success and achievement. Here the effort of standing and stooping to achieve is contrasted with an effortless prostration in respect. The teaching is that sometimes outward self-assertion regardless on what level--high (standing) or low (stooping)--does not yield the desired results. One, then, must turn inward and in profound respect for the wisdom of the ancestors as expressed in Ifa, surrender oneself to study and reflection. Having done this, one is then prepared to stand upright and step forward with a fresh energy and profound insight.

The metaphor of prostration in respect is an important one. It is at once a call for self-discipline and self-surrender. It is rooted in the Yoruba custom of bowing to the great, those great in age, great in wisdom or great in status. And thus, carries with it a need to recognize those who have achieved these positions of greatness. But in a deeper sense, it teaches us to be humble, to be willing to make oneself low in order to attain heights, to submit to instruction in order to learn and then be able to teach, and to open oneself in order to be filled.

ÌKÁ'GBE
36

36:1

He said it's a matter of disrespect.
I said it's a matter of being disregardful.
He said people dare not be so disrespectful of
fire that they would roll dry cloth in it.
I said people dare not be so disrespectful of a
snake that they would make it into a belt.
And they dare not be so disdainful towards
the child of a ruler
That they would strike him on the crown
of his head.
Thus, may people respect me likewise today
and always.

Ó ní: àfojúdi.
Mo ní: àfagbádi.
Ó ní: wọ́n kìí fojúdi iná kí wọ́n fi m'áṣọ ka.
Mo ní: wọ́n kìí fojúdi ejò kí wọ́n fi ṣ'ọ̀já.
Wọ́n kìí fojúdi ọmọ ọlọ́jà
Kí wọ́n kàn ní ìkó àtarí.
Kí wọ́n bù ọ̀wọ̀ fún mi l'oní àti nígbà gbogbo.

OGBÈ'TÚRÚPỌ̀N

37

37:1

Ogbe, bind your child securely on your back.
Nursing mother, firmly fix your child on it.
Carrying others' children is not as beneficial.
When a child cries out,
It is the mother whom we should inform.
This was the advice of Ifa for Adiro
Nigbagi-gbagi, the firmly fixed
hearthstone.
Who will sustain the wall without wavering.
She was advised to sacrifice.
It is when Adiro, the hearthstone, carries the
wall on its back,
That we have wealth,
That we have children,
That we have all good things.

OGBÈ'TÚRÚPỌ̀N

37

37:1

Ogbè, tún'mọ pọ̀n.
Abiyamọ sún'mọ sí.
Àgbàpọ̀n ni kò l'érè.
B'ọ́mọ bá ńké,
Ìyá làá wí fún.
Dífá fún Àdìrò Nigbagi-gbagi,
Ti yóó gbé ògiri pọ̀n tímọ́tímọ́.
Wọ́n níkí ó rúbọ.
Ó gbọ́; ó rúbọ.
Ìgbà Àdìrò gb'ógiri pọ̀n
La bá ń lájé,
La bá ńbímọ,
La bá ń níre gbogbo.

OGBÈ'TÚRÁ

39

39:1

If we have money and do not have character,
The money belongs to someone else.
Character, iwa, is what we are looking for,
character.
If we have children and do not have character,
The children belong to someone else.
Character, iwa, is what we are looking for,
character.
If we have a house and do not have character,
The house belongs to someone else.
Character, iwa, is what we are looking for,
character.
If we have clothes and do not have character,
The clothes belong to someone else.
Character, iwa, is what we are looking for,
character.
All the good things we have, if we do not have
character,
These good things belong to someone else.
And so, it's character, iwa, we are looking for,
character.

OGBÈ'TÚRÁ

39

39:1

Óní bó lówó, tá ò níwà,
Owó olówó ni.
Ìwà, ìwà l'a ńwá o, ìwà.
Ọmọ l'a bí, tá à níwà,
Ọmọ ọlọ́mọ ni.
Ìwà, ìwà l'a ńwá o, ìwà.
B'á a nílé, tá à níwà,
Ilé onìlé ni.
Ìwà, ìwà l'a ńwá o, ìwà.
B'á a l'áṣọ, tá à níwà,
Aṣọ aláṣọ ni.
Ìwà, ìwà l'a ńwá o, ìwà.
Ire gbogbo tá a ní,tá à níwà,
Ire oníre ni.
Ìwà, ìwà l'a ńwá o, ìwà.

39:2

Secret slander,
Undercover ridicule.
There is no one who turns his back
Who does not become the subject of slander.
This was the teaching for Orunmila
When people were directing slander against him.
He was advised to sacrifice.
He heard and he sacrificed.
He said: now, you may continue your slander,
But ridicule cannot remove the sweetness
from honey.
It is when you direct slander against me,
That I become extremely wealthy,
That I build houses upon houses,
That I bring into being an abundance of children,
And that I become the possessor of all
good things.
So, continue your slander,
For ridicule does not mean that honey will not
still be sweet.

39:2

Ṣùtisùti wúyẹwúyẹ.
Ṣùtisùti wúyẹwúyẹ.
Kò s'ẹ́ni ti yóo pẹ̀hìndà
Tí kò níí l'ọ́rọ̀ọ sùti l'ara.
Dífá fún Ọ̀rúnmìlà
Tí ọmọ aráyé yóò máa yọsùti síi.
Wọ́n níkí ó rúbọ.
Ó gbọ́; ó rúbọ
Ó ní: Ẹ ṣe máa yọsùti ẹ̀yin lọ
Ẹ̀gàn ò pé k'óyin má dùn.
Sùti lẹ yọ sí mi,
Ni mo fi lówó lọ́wọ́,
Ni mo fi kọ́lé mọ́lé,
Ni mo fi bímọ lé ọmọ,
Ni mo fi ní ire gbogbo.
Ẹ ṣe máa yọsùti ẹ̀yin lọ.
Ẹ̀gàn ò pé kóyin má dùn.

39:3

Anyone who wishes to have good fortune
Will constantly practice sacrifice.
And anyone who cultivates the habit of doing good deeds, especially for the needy,
This person, in particular, will never lack happiness.

Ẹnití ó bá sí ńwá ire,
L'ó màá ńṣ'ẹbọ.
Ẹnití ó bá sí fẹ́ràn ìwà oore ṣíṣe, pààpàá fún àwọn aláìní,
Oun paapaa kò ní yẹ̀ ní ìdùnú.

39:4

A person who is in deep distress cannot afford
to take an afternoon nap.
And a *useful* trap cannot afford to sleep at night.
This was the teaching of Ifa for Kosolu,
Offspring of Ojo; offspring of Owo;
The one who interpreted Ifa teachings
for Ininirin,
The offspring of the ruler of Orin-Abokun,
When she was continually suffering sickness
And looking forward to the day she would
rise up recovered.
They said she should sacrifice.
She heard and complied.

39:4

Ipọ́nripọ́njú ò sùn oorun ọ̀sán.
Ẹ̀bìtì kò sùn oorun òru.
Dífá fún Kósólu,
Ọmọ Ọjọ; ọmọ Ọ̀wọ;
Dífá fún Ìnínrín,
Ọmo Ọlọ́rin-Abòkun,
Níjọ́ tó ń ṣọ̀gbọ̀gbọ̀ àrùn
Tó ń najú àti díde.
Wọ́n níkí ó rúbọ.
Ó gbọ́; ó rúbọ.

39:5

A kindness done endures, but the foolish
person forgets it.
This was the teaching of Ifa for Igun
Who was going to give advice at the palace of
Olofin, *the ungrateful king*.
They said he should sacrifice.
He heard and he complied.
Igun, priest of the world, interpreted the
teachings of Ifa for the Olofin at Ife,
the cradle of the world,
When his life was broken like a calabash,
When it was torn completely apart like a
piece of cloth.
They said that he should sacrifice.
For he did not recognize Igun, the priest as
priest and respect him accordingly.

39:5

Olofin said he did not recognize Igun
any longer.
And he failed to recognize and respect
the priest as priest.
It is a kindness done which endures;
It is a foolish person who forgets it.

39:5

Oore pẹ́, asiwèrè gbàgbé.
Dífá fún Igún
Tí ńlọ gb'awo nílé Ọlọ́fin.
Wọ́n níkí ó rúbọ.
Ó gbọ́; ó rúbọ.
Igún, awo ayé,
Dífá fún Ọlọ́fin n'Ifẹ̀ Oòdáyé
Níjọ́ tí ayé rẹ̀ fọ́ bí igbá,
Tó fàya gbàràgàda bí aṣọ.
Wọ́n níkí ó rúbọ.
Ǹṣe lẹ ò m'awo l'áwo.
Ọlọ́fin l'ó un ò tún mọ Igún mọ́.
Ǹṣe lẹ ò m'awo l'áwo.
Oore l'ó pẹ́,
L'aṣiwèrè gbàgbé.

Ogbèatẹ̀

41

41:1

Even if the beginning of wrong-doing is pleasant,
The end of wickedness will not be good.
We cannot use evil to secure goods and expect them to be anchored firmly.
These were the teachings of Ifa for the upright one.
The offspring of the initiated one who treads the earth in humbleness.
Olodumare is the lord of the land.
Olodumare is the owner of judgment.
Retribution belongs to Olodumare.
The king of the world will reward everyone
Precisely according to the work of their hands.

Ogbèatẹ̀ 41

41:1

Bí iwájú ìkà bá dára,
Èyín ìkà kò níí sunwọ̀n.
A kìí fi ìkà di ẹrù kó gún gẹ́gẹ́.
Díá fún Òtítọ́-inú,
Ọmọ òtítẹ̀ afitẹlẹ̀ tìrẹlẹ̀tirẹlẹ̀.
Olódùmarè ló ní ilẹ̀.
Olódùmarè ló ní ídájọ́.
Ẹ́san ní ti Olódùmarè.
Ọ̀ba yóò san-án fún oníkálukú
Gẹ́gẹ́ bí iṣẹ́ ọwọ́ wọn.

41:2

T*he detractors said*, he would die in the forest,
But he was building mansions.
They said he would be buried in a hill of sand,
But he was accumulating and wearing
fine clothes.
They said that no one would assist him in
his work,
But he was dismounting male horses and
mounting female ones.
This was the teaching of Ifa for Orunmila,
When he was in the midst of enemies,
And when he was everyday engaged in
thoughts about doing battle.
They said he should practice sacrifice.
He heard and he complied.

41:2

Igbó ni yóò kú sí,
Ilé ǹláǹlá níí máa kọ́.
Òkè yẹ̀pẹ̀ ni yóò sùn,
Àkànpọ̀ ẹ̀wú jìmba-jìmba níí máa wọ̀.
Kò níí r'ẹ́nikan rán ní'ṣẹ́,
Látórí akọ ẹṣin níí tií bọ́ s'orí abo ẹṣin.
Dífá fún Ọ̀rúnmìlà
Nígbàtí o ńbẹ̀ níràngun ọ̀tá.
Ó f'ojoojúmọ́ kọminú ogun.
Wọ́n níkí ó rúbọ.
Ó gbọ́; ó rúbọ.

41:3

The gentle breeze causes leaves of the trees
on the farm to sway.
A strong wind shakes the leaves violently.
This was the teaching of Ifa for Orunmila.
Ifa said that the honor due me will be
shown to me.
Ifa asked me how prosperous would I like to be?
I said I would like to be as prosperous as
Olajugba of the city of Ilala.
Olajugba of Ilala turned a forest into a
dwelling place.
He turned a refuse site into a marketplace.
He built a home for his mother's family.
He built a house for his father's family.

41:3

He became a greatly respected person, one
whom upon waking one greets first.
He became a highly adored person,
one for whom people gather to praise.
May Ifa permit me to be as prosperous as
Olajugba of Ilala.

41:3

Aféfé lẹ́lẹ́ níí ṣ'ewe igi oko láálo-láálo.
Èfúùfù lẹ̀lẹ̀ níí ṣ'ewe igi oko gbáárikọ́kọ́-
gbáárikọ́ko.
Dífá fún Ọ̀rúnmìlà.
Ifá l'óun ó f'ọlá témi hàn mi.
Ifá ńi báwo ni ngo ṣe là tó .
Mo ní mo fé lálàálà bí Ọlájugbà Ìlàlà;
Ọlájugbà Ìlalà ló sọ igbó di ilé.
Ó s'àtàn d'ọjà.
Ó kọ́lẹ́ nílé íyá.
Ó kọ́lẹ́ nílé baba.
O di ẹni àjíkí.
Ó di ẹni àpèsìn.
Ifá jẹ́kí n là bí Ọlájugbà Ìlàlà.

41:4

Now, if I have been made,
I should reconstruct myself.
The forbidden things which are
enumerated for me,
I will comply with.
For I have been made,
And I must also remake myself.

Njẹ́ bí a bá tẹ̀ mi,
N ó tún'ra mi tẹ̀.
Èèwọ̀ tí a bá kà fún mi,
N ó gbọ́.
Titè l'a tẹ̀ mí,
N yóò tún'ra mi tẹ̀.

41:5

Let us close our eyes and pretend to be dead,
So that we may know who will mourn for us.
Let us walk unsteadily and pretend to stumble,
So that we might see who will express concern.
It would not be a bad thing, even if we could
count on only one person.
But who will remain is difficult to determine.
This was the teaching of Ifa for Orunmila
When he was going to make people think
that he was dead,
So that he might know who were his true friends.
He was advised to sacrifice.
He heard and he complied.

41:5

Orunmila who was said to be dead was not
dead after all.
He discovered that their mourning was a
mourning for themselves.
And their fasting in sorrow was a fasting
for themselves.
Only his true friends remained to mourn him
and help his family.

41:5

K'a dijú, k'á pé a kú,
K'a m'ẹnití yóó sunkún ẹni.
K'a bùrìn-bùrìn, k'á kọsẹ̀ dánwò,
K'a mọ̀ ẹnití yóò ṣeni pẹ̀lẹ́.
Kò ní burúburú bí kó má kẹnìkan péré mọ́ ni.
Ṣúgbọ́n ẹnití yóò kù l'a ò mọ̀.
Dífá fún Ọ̀rúnmìlà
Nígbàtí ó ńfi ikú tàn wọ́n jẹ,
Kí ó mọ̀ ẹnití ńbẹ ọ̀rẹ́ olóòótọ́ rẹ̀.
Wọ́n níkí ó rúbọ.
Ó gbọ́; ó rúbọ.
Ọ̀rúnmìlà ní e pé a kú kò kú mọ́ o.
Ó wá rí pé ẹkún ara wọn ni wọ́n ńsun.
Pé àrùwè ara wọn ni wọ́n ńgba.
Àwọn ọ̀rẹ́ olóòótọ́ rẹ̀ ńikan ní ńbẹ l'éhìn
tí ńsunkún àti tí ńran àwọn ara rẹ lọ́wọ́.

41:5

ÀSỌYÉ

This is a teaching on the test and discovery of friendship. The narrative from which this teaching comes tells us that Orunmila was being greatly praised by persons and people who were claiming a friendship with him and yet he felt uneasy about the sincerity of the praise and the quality of his friends. So, he pretended to die so that he could test the sincerity and commitment of the people. Once the pretenders heard he was dead, they collected monies from his family unjustly, did not help the family, mourned falsely and disrespected his memory. But some people who never made outrageous claims nor promised great things came to truly mourn his passing and to help his family with all that was necessary. They were ready to stay 40 days for mourning, but Orunmila returned on the 7th day. When the pretenders heard Orunmila had returned, they came to ask for forgiveness.

But they had already revealed themselves! It was his true friends to whom he turned in reciprocity and even deeper respect.

The lesson here is that true friends not only aid and praise each other in each other's presence, but also demonstrate in each other's absence an equal or even greater commitment to the friendship. This is a situation, our ancestors in ancient Egypt say, in which one friend's righteousness and goodness equal the other's. It is thus, balanced, mutually beneficial and worthy of the highest sacrifice.

41:6

Unhelpful persons are as abundant
as bushes in the forest.
A good person is as rare as another eye.
To find a good person, one must travel
a long way.
These were the teachings of Ifa for Orunmila
When he was going to become husband
of the world,
When he was going to share the world into
two equal parts with Olodumare.
He was advised to practice sacrifice.
He heard and he practiced it.

41:6

Ènìyàn lásan pọ́ bí ìgbẹ́.
Ẹnirere wọ́n ju ojú lọ.
K'á tó rí ẹnirere, ọ̀nà á jìn.
Dífá fún Ọ̀rúnmìlà
Nígbàtí ó ńlọ rèé ṣ'ọkọ ayé,
Ó ńlọ rèé bá Olódùmarè pín ayé lọ́gbọọgba.
Wọ́n níkí ó rúbọ.
Ó gbọ́; ó rúbọ

41:6

ÀSỌYÉ

This is a teaching on accepting responsibility for the world we live in and knowing both the difficulty and the honor. The honor is to be *husband of the world* or *wife of the world* and to share this responsibility with the Lord of Heaven, Olodumare. This status and role as husband or wife of the world, *ọkọ ayé* or *aya ayé,* calls for all the virtues of marriage - love, respect, care, commitment, partnership, sacrifice, shared work, shared joy, shared life. The second aspect of this role and status is to be partner with the Lord of Heaven in care and responsibility for the world. This reaffirms the divine character of the role and status and reaffirms the teaching in Odu 78 that says "surely humans have been chosen to bring good into the world." This adds the dimension that this bringing of good into the world is in partnership with the Divine.

It is important here to note that Kawaida

recognizes the specific assignment which is given to Orunmila, to be husband of the world. But it sees this teaching in its larger meaning as an assignment for all humans in the model of Orunmila. Thus, it is the Ifa teachings that are both husband and wife of the world and serve in partnership with Olodumare in giving indispensable moral and spiritual vision and values to the world through Olodumare's assignment. For to rightly and effectively assume responsibility and care for the world requires the highest spiritual and moral vision and values.

Finally, the text says that useless or unhelpful persons are everywhere, but one must travel far to find a good person. This is a teaching that in carrying out one's responsibility one must realize that only a few will be immediately useful to the task of bringing good into the world. It is important to notice that the world *lásan* or useless is used here to describe the many rather than evil as in some traditions. It therefore does not challenge the concept of our chosenness. It speaks to our *usefulness* or *non-usefulness* as human beings in carrying out the task of bringing good into the world at any given time. And it challenges us by implication to dare to be those rare and precious good persons caring to constantly lift up the light that lasts, those eternal moral and spiritual principles of our ancestors as expressed in the teachings of Ifa. For through this, we open the way for others so that the truly good persons are no longer rare, but are regular everyday people and everywhere.

OGBÈ'ṢẸ́

43

43:1

Even if we are going to die,
We must wage a life-and-death struggle.
We should still struggle hard.
This was the teaching of Ifa for the lame person.
And the same was given to the blind person.
They said that both should sacrifice.
They heard and they complied.
Before long and not too far in the future, then,
You can come and join us where practicing
sacrifice produces victory.

Bí a yió kúu,
A yió jòwèrè.
A yió jòwèrè.
Dífá fún arọ.
A bù fún afọ́jú.
Wọ́n ní kí àwọn méjèèjì rúbọ.
Wọ́n gbọ́; wọ́n rúbọ.
Kò pẹ́, kọ̀ jínnà,
Ẹ wá bá'ni ní àrúṣẹ́ ogun.

43:2

I pursue the work my destiny has assigned me.
I follow the path down which Ifa directs me.
This was the teaching of Ifa for Agbonbula,
Who would drain the deepest waters in order to be prosperous.
They said he should practice sacrifice.
He heard and he complied.
I will not fail to drain the deepest waters in order to be prosperous.
I will not fail to drain the deepest waters to achieve goodness.

43:2

Iṣẹ́ orí rán mi ni mò ńṣe o.
Ọ̀nà Èdu rán mi ni mò ńtọ̀.
Dífá fún Agbọ́nbúla
Tí yóó gbọ́n ibú là.
Wọ́n níkí ó rúbọ.
Ó gbọ́; ó rúbọ.
N kò ṣai gbọ́n ibú mi là.
N kò ṣai gbọ́n ibú mi níre.

Ọ̀SẸ́ ÓGBÈ
44

44:1

Orunmila says that we should endure
hardship in the beginning,
So that we might enjoy prosperity in the end.

Ọ̀rúnmìlà níkí a ìbá fòsì síwájú
K'á f'ọrọ̀ s'ẹ̀hin.

Ogbè Ofún
45

45:1

I made a small sacrifice,
And it yielded a small result.
This was the teaching of Ifa for Iya Ajija,
When she was crying and complaining
That she could not achieve any good.
They said she should sacrifice.
She heard and she made the sacrifice.

Mo rú kéré.
Ó dá kéré.
Dífá fún Ìyá Àjíjà,
Ó ńmójú ẹkún sun ráhùn
Kí ó kò lè ṣe tán ni ire gbogbo.
Wọ́n níkí ó rúbọ.
Ó gbọ́; ó rúbọ.

ÌDÍ'YẸ̀KÚ 50

50:1

The way of Ifa is very straight.
It does not deviate.
This was the teaching of Ifa for Oye,
When he was going to marry a bride
from his own neighborhood.
They said he should sacrifice,
So that his penis would not put him to shame.
But Oye would not sacrifice.
So when he took his wife home,
He could not sleep with her.
They said that Oye had died at the waist.
Ifa says a person should sacrifice against
diseases which can be concealed
under one's clothes.

ÌDÍ'YẸKÚ
50

50: I

Ọnà Ifá tọ tààrà.
Kò yà.
A dá fún Ọ̀yẹ́,
Nígbàtí ó nlọ gbé ìyàwó adúgbò wá ilé.
Wọ́n níkí ó rúbọ,
Kí ọkó rẹ̀ má ba dójútì oun.
Ọ̀yẹ́ kò rúbọ.
Nígbàtí Ọ̀yẹ mú ìyàwó délé,
Kò lè basùn.
Wọ́n ní Ọ̀yẹ tí ó ti kú ní ìdí ni.
Ifá ní kí ẹníkan rúbo àrùn, a fi aṣọ bò mọ́ra.

ỌYẸKÚ ỌKÀNRÀN
57

57:1

On the day that Olodumare would think
that a star was being arrogant,
We would see that star suddenly fall and
disappear into darkness.

Ni ọjọ́ tí Olódùmarè bá rò
Ti ìgbéraga ìràwọ̀ kan,
Ni a ṣe nríí tí ìràwọ̀ náà ṣídìí lójijì
a sì wọ òòkún.

65:1

Orunmila will forgive me.
The forgiving one will forgive me.
If water kills a person, people will forgive it.
Orunmila, may people forgive me in this matter,
Even as the entire town usually forgives rain.

Ọ̀rúnmìlà fihun jìmí
Ojìjì fihun jìmi.
Bí omi bá pọ'ni, wọ́n á fijìí.
Ọ̀rúnmìlà, kí wọ́n f'ọ̀ràn yìí jìmí,
Bí gbogbo ilú níí f'ọ̀ràn jì òjò.

ÌRẸTẸ̀'YẸ̀KÚ
70

70:1

Orifusi, father of Elu, was searching
for a way to avoid death.
So that death would not kill him, his children
and his wives,
They said: if you want to avoid death,
You must sacrifice and follow the
teachings of Ifa.
Ifa will teach you the conduct and character
Which will enable you to avoid death.
They said when you sacrifice, you should
begin doing good from this day on
more than ever before.
For your sacrifice is in vain, if your character
is deficient.

70:1

Therefore, you should take the sacrificial
pigeons and chickens home.
You should release them.
You should not kill them.
You should give them food, if they come
to eat at your house.
And you must not kill anything whatsoever
from this day on.
For one who does not want death to kill him,
Should not kill anything whatsoever either.

ÌRẸTẸ̀'YẸ̀KÚ
70

70:1

Orifusi baba Elu ńwá ibi a bá yẹ̀ ìkú,
Sí kí ó ma lè pa òun,ọmọ rẹ̀ ti aya rẹ̀.
A níkí bí ẹ bá wípé kí ikú má lè pa ẹ̀yin,
Kí ẹ rúbọ kí ẹ sì wá tẹ Ifá.
Ifá yóò má kó ẹ̀yin, ní ìṣe àti ìwà
Tí kìí jékií a kú.
Wọ́n ní bí ẹ rúbọ,
Ẹ bẹ̀rẹ̀sí rere-ìṣe láti oní lọ jù ti àtẹ̀hìn wá.
Lásan ni ẹ rúbọ, bí ẹ bá dín ìwàrere.
Kí ẹ kó àwọn ẹyẹlé àti adìyẹ lọ sí ilé ẹ̀yin.
Kí ẹ kó wọn dàsílẹ̀.
Kí ẹ má ṣe pa wọn.
Kí ẹ máa fún wọn ni oúnjẹ bí wọ́n bá jẹ wá ilé.
Ẹ kò gbódò pa ohunkóhun láti oní lọ.
Nítorí ẹnitì kò fẹ́ kí ikú pa òun,
Kí ó má ṣe ikú pa ohunkóhun sì.

70:2

May death not ruin my house.
I have not done evil.
May disease not ruin my house.
I have not done evil.
Whether enemy or friend, I have shown them kindness.
I have not done evil.
When people were engaged in litigation at Ake,
I was compassionate and I was kind to them.
When people were involved in lawsuits at Oko,
I was compassionate and I showed them kindness.
I have not done evil.
May litigation not ruin my house.
I have not done evil.

70:2

When I found two people fighting,
I mediated between them.
I have not done evil.
May poverty not ruin my house.
I dare not be lazy.
May loss not ruin my house.
I dare not steal.

70:2

Ikú má sọ'lé mi d'ode.
N kò má ṣìkà.
Àrùn má sọ'lé mi d'ode.
N kò má ṣìkà.
Àti ọ̀tá ati ọ̀ré, mo ṣe wọ́n lóore.
N kò má ṣìkà.
Ẹjọ́ bá wọn l'Ákẹ́,
Mo dáròdárò; mo ṣe wọ́n lóore.
N kò má ṣìkà.
Ẹjọ́ bá wọn l'Oko,
Mo dáròdárò; mo ṣe wọ́n lóore.
N kò má ṣìkà.
Ẹjọ́ má sọ'lé mi d'ode.
N kò má ṣìkà.
Mo bá ẹníkẹjì ńjà,
Mo là wọ́n ní ìjà.
N kò má ṣìkà.
Òṣì má ṣ'ọ̀lẹ̀ mi d'ode.
N kò jẹ́ sọ̀'lé
Òfò má sọ'lé mi d'ode.
N kò jẹ́ jalè.

ỌYẸ̀KÚ Ọ̀ṢẸ́
71

71:1

The teachings of Ifa were interpreted for the
wise ones.
Who assembled and invited some babalawo to
interpret the teachings of Ifa on death.
They asked "Why is it that death kills people
and there is no one who does not die?"
The babalawo said that Ifa says it is good
that Amuniwaye, the One who brought us
into the world, created death.
Water which does not flow back and forth
Becomes a pond of polluted water, a pond of
water which causes disease.
Water takes people away freely and water
brings them back freely.
Let the ill go home to receive a new body;

ÒYẸ̀KÚ Ọ̀ṢẸ́
71

71:1

Let the corrupt go home to receive
new character;
So they may return to the world.
The babalawo then asked:
"What is unpleasant about this?"
The wise ones bowed in respect for Ifa, saying:
The offering has been made; may it be accepted;
and may it be blessed.
Then, they dispersed and went away.
And they no longer regarded death as a matter
of sorrow.

Ọ̀YẸ̀KÚ Ọ̀ṢẸ́
71

71:1

A dífá fún àwọn amòye,
Ti wọ́n gbárá jọ ńpè babaláwo wá dífá ikú.
Wọ́n ní: èétirí ikú fi ńpọ'ni tí kòsí ẹnití kíí kù?
Àwọn babaláwo ní: Ifá wípé ire li
Amuniwáyé ńfi ìkú ṣe.
Omi tí kò sàn síwájú tí kò padà sẹ́hin
Á dọ̀gọdọ̀ omi ìbàjẹ̀, ọ̀gọ̀dọ̀ omi àrùn
Omi ńgbé wọn lo réré; omi ńkó wọn bọ̀ réré.
Olókùrùn k'á re'lé lọ gba àwọ̀ titun;
Asẹ̀bàjẹ́ k'á re'lé lọ gbà ìwà titun;
Kí wọ́n bọ̀wá'yé.
Àwọn babaláwo ní: èwo ni kò dùn?
Àwọn amòye foríbalẹ̀ fún Ifá ńwípé:
Ọ̀rúnmìlà, aború; boyè; bọṣíṣẹ́.
Wọ́n túka lọ.
Wọ́n kò gbà ikú sí ọ̀ràn ẹ̀dùn mọ́.

ÌWÒRÌ ÒDÍ

75

75:1

There is no childbearing woman who
cannot give birth to an Ifa priest.
There is no childbearing woman who cannot
give birth to Orunmila, himself.
Our father, if he fully brings us into being,
Eventually we will bring him into being.
Our mother, if she fully gives birth to us,
Eventually, we will give birth to her.
This was the teaching of Ifa for Orunmila,
Who said he would bring heaven to earth,
And he would take earth to heaven.

ÌWÒRÌ ÒDÍ
75

75:1

Kòsí abiyamọ tí kò lé bí awo l'ọmọ.
Kòsí abiyamọ tí kò lé bí Ọ̀rúnmìlà.
Baba ẹni bí ó bá bíni ní pépé,
Bí ó bá pẹ́ títí á tún ńbí baba ẹni lọ́mọ
Yèyé ẹni bí ó bá bíni ní pépé,
Bí ó bá pẹ́ títí á tún nbí yèyé ẹni lọ́mo
A dífá fún Ọ̀rúnmìlà,
Ti ọ́ wípé òun máà mú ọ̀run bọ̀ sáyé
Òun máà mù ayé lọ ṣọ́run.

ÌDÍ'WÒRÌ

76

76:1

It is Ela Iwori who will not allow the world
to be ruined.
When the world of Oba'lufe fell into disorder,
It was Ela Iwori who restored order to it.
When the commitment breakers in Akila
corrupted the town,
It was Ela Iwori who set things right again
for the people.
When day turned into night in the city
of Okerekese,
When conditions in this city became chaotic,
And when the priests there failed to find
a solution,
It was Ela Iwori who helped Oluyori,
the King there, to set things right again.

ÌDÍ'WÒRÌ
76

76:1

When Elegbara plans to turn the world
    upside down,
It is Ela Iwori who blocks his way.
Ela Iwori does not accept money.
Ela Iwori does not accept kola nuts.
And yet, it is he who sets right unfortunate
    destinies.

76:1

Ẹ̀là Ìwòrì ní kìí jẹ́kí ayé ra'jú.
Nígbàtí ayé Ọba'Lufe dàrú,
Ẹ̀là Ìwòrì l'ó báa tún ayé rẹ̀ ṣe.
Nígbàtí àwọn ọ̀dàlè ìlú Akilà bà ayé
ìlú wọn jẹ́,
Ẹ̀là Ìwòrì l'ó bá wọ́n tún un ṣe.
Nígbàtí ọ̀sán d'òru ni ìlú Ọ̀kẹ̀rẹ̀kẹ̀sẹ̀,
Ti ayé ìlú náà di rúdurùdu,
Ti àwọn awo ìbẹ̀ bàtì,
Ẹ̀là Ìwòrì l'ó bá Olúyorí Ọba ìbẹ̀ tún un ṣe.
Nígbàtí Ẹlẹ́gbára bá nfẹ́ ṣ'orí ayé kodò,
Ẹ̀là Ìwòrì ni máà dúbùú ọ̀nà rẹ̀.
Ẹ̀là Ìwòrì kìí gbowó.
Ẹ̀là Ìwòrì kìí gbobì.
Òun ló sì ńtún orí ti kò sunwọ̀n ṣe.

76:2

If we have wisdom and do not use it,
We will become uninformed persons.
If we have ability and do not use it,
We will become sluggish.
This was the teaching of Ifa for people
Who were not associating with the wise,
nor with the worker;
And who were forging friendships with
the unworthy of the world.
Ifa reprimanded them saying:
You are not associating with good people.
You are not keeping company with persons
of worth.
And this usually brings misfortune to people.

76:2

Bí a lọ́gbọ́n nínú bí a kò lòó,
A ó d'ọ̀gbẹ̀rì.
Bí a lágbára nínú bí a kò lòó,
A ó d'ọ̀le.
A dífá fún àwọn ènìyàn,
Tí wọ́n má b'ọlọ́gbọ́n rin má b'aṣiṣẹ
Ti wọ́n ṣọ̀ọ̀ré èrò ìsàlẹ̀ ayé.
Ifá ńbá wọn wí ó ní:
Ìwọ kò bá enirere rìn.
Ìwọ kò bá enirere ṣọ̀rẹ́.
Orí burúkú níí mú bá ènìyàn.

ÌWÒRÌ'ROSÙ
77

77:1

When a new day dawns we should not be as
uniformed as yesterday.
This was the teaching of Ifa for Komo,
the uninformed one,
Who was meditating on how he should have
done something yesterday.
He meditated until he fell asleep.
When the day dawned and twilight appeared,
He still did not know for certain what
he should have done.
Therefore, we should strive day after day
to accomplish a task.
And if that is not enough, then we should strive
month after month to succeed,
Until eventually we know what we should do.
They said he should sacrifice so that
his plans would prosper.
He heard and practiced sacrifice.

Ìwòrì'Rosù

77

77:1

Bí ojúmó bá nmọ́, a kò nii y'ọ̀gbẹrí bí ọjọ àná.
Ni ó dífá fún Kòmọ̀,
Tí ó ńronú bí oun tí máà ṣe kiní yi sí lánàá.
Ó ronú títí ó sùn.
Nígbàtí ojúmọ́ mọ́ ti ọ̀yẹ́ là,
Kò ìmọ èyítí òun máà ṣe dandan.
Njẹ́ kí a jẹ́kí ọjọ bọrí ọjọ́.
Bí kò bá tó, kí oṣù bọ́rí oṣù,
Bópẹ́títí aó mọ̀ eyíti á máà ṣe.
Wọ́n níkí ó rúbọ, kí èro rẹ̀ má ṣe orí.
Ó gbọ́; ó rúbọ.

Ìrosù Wòrì

78

78:1

Let us do things with joy.
Those who want to go, let them go.
Those who want to stay, let them stay.
Surely, humans have been chosen to bring
good into the world.
The All-Knowing One, priest of Orunmila,
interpreted the teachings of Ifa
for Orunmila.
He said the people of the world would come
to ask him a certain question.
He said that Orunmila should sacrifice.
Orunmila heard and complied.
One day all kinds of people, good people and
those who do not allow good in other
people's lives gathered together.
They then went to Orunmila.
They said: "Coming back and forth to earth
tires us, Orunmila.
Therefore, please allow us to rest in heaven."

ÌROSÙ WÒRÌ

78

78:1

Orunmila said: "You cannot avoid going
back and forth to earth,
Until you bring about the good condition that
Olodumare has ordained for every
human being.
After then, you may rest in heaven.
They asked "What is the good condition?"
Orunmila said: "The good condition is a
good world:
A world in which there is full knowledge
of all things;
Happiness everywhere;
Life without anxiety or fear of enemies;
Without clashes with snakes or other
dangerous animals;
Without fear of death, disease, litigation
losses, wizards, witches or Eshu;
Without fear of injury from water or fire; and
Without fear of poverty or misery.

ÌROSÙ WÒRÌ
78

78:1

Because of your wisdom, your compelling
desire for good character and your
internal strength.
The things needed to bring about the good
condition in the world then are:
Wisdom that is fully adequate to
govern the world;
Sacrifice; character; the love of doing good
for all people, especially those who are in
need,
And those who seek assistance from us;
And the eagerness and struggle to increase
good in the world,
And not let any good at all be lost.
People will continue to go to heaven;
And they will go back and forth to earth after
their transfiguration,
Until everyone has achieved the good condition.
Thus, when the children of Oduduwa gather
together,
Those chosen to bring good into the world are
called human beings or the chosen ones.

ÌROSÙ WÒRÌ
78

78:1

K'á fi'núdídùn ṣeé.
Ẹní máa lọ, kí ó máa lọ.
Ẹní máa dẹ̀hìn, kí ó máa dẹ̀hìn.
Dandan,ènìyàn ni a yàn kí wọ́n mú're lọ sáyé.
Mọ̀ràntan awo Ọ̀rúnmìlà l'o dífá f' Ọ̀rúnmìlà.
Ó ní àwọn ọmọ-ayé ńbọ̀wá bíléèrè ọ̀rọ̀ kan.
A níkí Ọ̀rúnmìlà rúbọ.
Ọ̀rúnmìlà gbọ́; ó rúbọ.
Nijọ́kan onírúurú ènìyàn, àwọn ènìyàn rere àti
àwọn ènìyàn má jẹ́kí l'ènìyàn sunwọ̀n
gbárajo.
Wọ́n tọ̀ Ọ̀rúnmìlà wá.
Wọ́n ní ìpaarà ayé yí sú wa Ọ̀rúnmìlà.
Nítorínáà, kí ó jọ̀wọ́ jẹ́kí a simi sí ọ̀run.
Ọ̀rúnmìlà ní ẹyin kò lè sàì máà paara òde-ayé,
Títí ẹyin yóò fi dé ipò rere náà tí Olódùmarè ti
yàn fún gbogbo ènìyàn.
Lẹ̀hìnnáà ni ẹyin yóò simi sí ọ̀run.

ÌROSÙ WÒRÌ
78

78:1

Wọ́n ní: kíni ipò rere?
Ọ̀rúnmìlà ní ipò rere náà li ayé rere:
Ayé àmotán ohun gbogbo;
Ayọ̀ níbi-gbogbo;
Wìwà láìsí ominú tàbí ìbẹrù ọ̀tá;
Láìsí íjà ejò tàbí ẹranko búburú míràn;
Láìsí ìbẹ̀rù ìkú, àrùn, ẹjọ́, òfù, oṣó, ajẹ́ tàbí Èṣù;
Láìsí ìbẹ̀rù ìfarapa omi tàbí iná;
Àti láìsí ìbẹ̀rù àìní tàbí òṣì,
Nítorí ọgbón, yún ìwàrere àti agbára inú.
Ohun tí yóò gbé wá dé ipò rere náà:
Ọgbón tí ó pọ̀ tọ́ eyítí a lè fiṣe àkóso ayé;
Ìrubọ́, ìwà, ìfẹ́ran oore-ṣíṣe fún gbogbo
 ènìyàn, ni pàtàkì jùlọ àwọn ti iṣe aláìní,
Àti àwọn tí ó ńfẹ́ íràǹlọ́wọ́ lọ́dọ̀ wa;
Ìtara fún ati sísà ipá láti fi kún ire tí ó
 wà ni ayé;

ÌROSÙ WÒRÌ
78

78: I

Láìjẹ́kí ire èyíkéyìí tí a ti ní lọ.
Àwọn ènìyàn yóó máà lọ sí ọ̀run.
Wọ́n yóò sì máà padà wá s'óde ayé
léhín ìparadà wọ́n,
Títí ẹnìkọ̀ọ̀kan yóó fi dé ipò rere náà.
Nítorínáà nígbàtí àwọn ọmọ Odùduà pé jọ,
Àwọn tí ó yàn láti kó ire wá s'óde ayé ni
à ńpè ní: ènìyàn.

ÌROSÙ'WÒRÌ
78

78:1

ÀSỌYÉ

No Odu and ese is more definitive of the rich and varied range and depth of the moral concerns and instructions of the Odu Ifa than Odu Irosu'Wori (78:1). Its richness, range and depth are rooted in a moral anthropology , a conception of the human person and the meaning and mission of human life, which is of profound human significance, both in a personal and collective sense. At the heart of Ifa moral anthropology is the teaching that humans are *chosen* by the Creator to bring good into the world and that this special status and task are the fundamental mission and meaning of human life. In fact, the central word for human in Yoruba is *ènìyàn*, which literally means the *chosen ones*. This fact not only stresses the moral significance of this status, but also is a clear and constant point of reference in our understanding and treatment of human beings. This concept of "chosenness" is significant in several ways. First, it represents the highest level of ethical humanism in its conception of *all* humans as chosen (*yàn*) without distinction of nation, gender, race, ethnicity, class or a special religious relationship or promise. It, thus, poses the ideal many other world religions are still trying to establish as a central moral doctrine.

Secondly, this moral and spiritual conception of the human person is important because it is a chosenness endowed by the Creator with all the transcendent and ultimate meaning this brings with it for us as persons, peoples and members of the human community. Thirdly, the special status of human as chosen ones (*ènìyàn*) is a companion concept of our being *ọmọ Olódùmarè*, the offspring of Olodumare, God. It, thus, reinforces the Ifa concept that we are in the image of God and gives augmented grounding to the concept of our inherent and inviolable worthiness which we call human dignity. This moral sense of inherent worthiness of the human person is reflected throughout the Odu in instructions to respect all persons and in the constant concerns for honor, dignity and respect, and the need to reaffirm, defend and maintain these. The various words for these concerns are *ọlá, ìyìn* and *ọ̀wọ̀* which may be used to indicate both inherent and socially achieved and recognized worthiness.

The significance of the Ifa concept of chosenness rests also in its role of adding an active dimension to the spiritual and moral understanding of what it means to be in the image of God. For it requires that the image not be one simply of *spiritual origin* as divine offspring but also one of *moral action* as bringers-of-Good-in-the-world in emulation of the Creator. Therefore, being in the image of God or like God is not only an affirmation of inherent worth or dignity but also a certain way of asserting oneself in the world.

The Odu begins by teaching us that, as the chosen ones, we should do things with joy. This speaks not only to the happiness we should experience in our divine designation and assignment, but also to the Ifa conception of the world as essentially good but constantly needing to be renewed and enriched with added good. Secondly, the text speaks to the issue of free will in its apparent suggestion that we may accept and engage in our divinely assigned task and honor our special status or not. Clearly, there are consequences throughout the Odu for those who reject or act in contradiction to our divine chosenness. But we can and must choose even as we are chosen.

Also, the value of this text is expressed in its affirmation that the Creator has not only chosen humans as bringers-of-good-in-the-world, but also has ordained that each and every human being should enjoy a *good life* in a *good world*. In fact, the text says that not only should we have a good life in the world, but also that we are the ones who must bring the good world into being which makes the good life possible. The question is then posed to the sage and master teacher, Orunmila, what is a good life, called here the good condition or position, *ipò rere*? And Orunmila answers by saying that the achieving of a good life is the achieving of a good world defined by several essential things: knowledge of all things; universal happiness; freedom from anxiety and fear of hostile others; the end of antagonism with other beings on earth, i.e., animals, reptiles and the like; well-being and the end of fear of forces that threaten it, and finally, freedom from poverty and misery.

At this point the text reaffirms the idea of human *agency*, i.e., our moral capacity and need to think, feel and act as competent and concerned beings, which is so essential to concepts of what it means to be human as well as what it means to be moral. Indeed, it tells us that the good world requires ongoing effort from us for its achievement. The text first sums up the requirements as: "wisdom, the compelling desire for good character and internal strength" or the power of will. This stress on wisdom, which is repeated, reaffirms the importance of knowledge in the Ifa ethical tradition and reminds us that the first condition required for a good world is knowledge --full and varied and in every realm. The text, however, goes on to give us a longer list. This includes again wisdom, but further defines it as "wisdom to adequately govern the world."

This, of course, reaffirms human responsibility for the world (Odu 33:2) and the need to be wise enough to carry out the responsibility effectively. Here the core wisdom is, of necessity, moral and spiritual wisdom which conceives of the world in its interrelated wholeness, respects its integrity and works constantly to save, renew and expand the good in it. But it also means that we must know the world in its concreteness and wholeness and thus requires human development and mastery of all the disciplines of human knowledge. A similar stress on the possession of knowledge as a defining characteristic of humans and its need for full realization of our humanity is found in ancient Egyptian moral teachings. In fact, a central word for humans in ancient Egyptian is *rḫyt*, "possessors of knowledge" or "knowing beings."

Character, the relatively stable disposition toward doing good and right, is also reaffirmed as an indispensable aspect of being moral and bringing good into the world. Moreover, the text lists also as essential to this moral project, sacrifice, and love of good doing, especially for the needy and those who ask. And finally, it further defines the needs of the project and the project itself of bringing good into the world as "*the eagerness and an ongoing struggle to increase good in the world and not let any good be lost.*"

In sum, then, what is needed are: wisdom, character, sacrifice, good-doing, commitment, struggle--and of course--a self-understanding of our chosenness that undergirds and encourages our self-conscious and effective assertion in the world. These seven themes appear repeatedly throughout the Odu Ifa and form the core concepts of what it means to be moral and act morally in the Ifa ethical tradition. This Odu and ese, then, serve as a central source for understanding Ifa ethics and thus warrant this more extensive Asoye and continuous study and reflection.

78:2

If we continually tasted sweetness without
tasting a little bitterness also,
Life would be dull.
One who has never experienced the
hardship of adversity,
Does not really know the pleasure of prosperity.
This was the teaching of Ifa for a group
of farmers,
Who said that if all seasons were just the
rainy season,
The world would be immeasurably pleasant.
They said they would offer sacrifice
So that Orunmila might graciously help them.
Orunmila said that they should instead sacrifice
because of their foolishness.
And that the world should remain as Oduduwa
has created it.

78:2

So that the rainy season and the dry season
will not fail to come.
They would not sacrifice.
Orunmila then allowed the rains to pour down
continuously that year,
So that there was not even a glimpse of the sun.
People began to become ill.
And many of them died that year.
Also crops and the like did not fare well.
The people returned to sacrifice and pray.
Orunmila said to them: ashes rise;
The sacrifice must be doubled.

78:2

Bí a jẹ adùn títí láìjẹ ìkorò díè sìì,
Ayé a máa sú nii jẹ .
Ẹnití kò jẹ ìpónjú rí,
Kò mọ̀ adùn ọrọ̀.
A dífá fún àwọn àgbẹ̀ tí nwípé:
Gbogbo ìgbà ayé ibá jẹ kìkì òjò
Ayé ibá dùn adùntán.
Wọ́n ní àwọn a rúbọ
Ki Ọ̀rúnmìlà jọ̀wọ́ yéé gbà wọ́n.
Ọ̀rúnmìlà ní kí wọ́n wá rúbọ nítorí íwèrè wọn.
Àti pé kí ayé lè maa wà bí Odùdúwà tí dá ayé sì,
Ìgbà òjò àti ígbà èèrún kí ó má tàsé.
Wọ́n kò rúbọ.
Ọ̀rúnmìlà wá jẹ́kí òjò rọ́ púpò li ọdún náà títí.
A kò fi rí òòrùn rárá.

78:2

Ènìyàn bẹ̀rẹ̀si s'ọ̀kùnrùn.
Wọ́n sì kú púpọ̀ nínú ọdún náà.
Ohun-ọ̀gbìn àti bẹẹbẹẹ kọ̀ dára.
Wọ́n padà wá rúbọ pẹ̀lú ẹbẹ.
Ọ̀rúnmìlà ni: ẹ̀rú gọ̀kẹ̀.
Ẹbọ l'ó sọdi méjì.

80:1

Yams were scarce; palm oil was scarce;
corn was scarce.
All food items were in short supply.
The teachings of Ifa were interpreted for
the people of Iwori.
They said that the people should sacrifice,
So that they might have abundance.
They heard and they sacrificed.
The babalawo said that all the people should
gather their hoes and cutlasses,
And go work on the farms,
So that abundance might come for them.
For only work alleviates adversity.

80:1

Isú wọ́n; epó wọ́n; àgbàdo wọ́n.
Ohun gbogbo tí ẹnú njẹ ni ó wọ́n.
A dífá fún wọ́n l'óde Ìwòrì.
Wọ́n níkí wọ́n rúbọ kí ọ̀pọ̀ lè dé fún wọ́n.
Wọ́n gbọ́; wọ́n rúbọ.
Babaláwo níkí gbogbo ènìyàn kó ọkọ́ àti àdá,
Kí wọ́n máa re oko lọ ṣiṣé,
Kí ọ̀pọ̀ lè dé.
Iṣẹ́ ní ídẹ ìpọ́njú.

ỌBÀRÀ'WÒRÌ

82

82:1

Heavy words have the weight of an anvil.
This was the teaching of Ifa for the world,
At a time when all the people of the world
were overpraising money saying:
There is nothing else in the world that is
more respected than money.
They said they would give up everything,
And they would continuously run after money.
Orunmila said: what you think about
money is so.
And what you think about money is also not so.
It is the teachings of Ifa we should honor.
It is these we should regard highly.
It is said money is a raiser of status and a
corrupter of character.
A person who loves money excessively,
his character will be ruined.
Good character is the finest beauty of a person.

Ọ̀BÀRÀ'WÒRÌ
82

82:1

Even if you have money, it does not mean
you will not become blind.
It does not mean you will not go mad.
It does not mean you will not become lame.
It does not mean you will not become ill
and the like.
You still can become disabled in any
part of your body.
Therefore you should go and get more wisdom
So that you may think deeply about things.
You should cultivate good character;
You should acquire wisdom;
And you should come and sacrifice
So that you may be at ease inside and out.

82:1

Ọ̀rọ̀ bàntà a wúwo bí owú.
A dífá fún ayé,
Níjọ́ tí gbogbo ọmọ arayé npọ́n owó pé:
Kòsí ohun míràn mọ́ nínú ayé tí ó tún
ní iyì mọ́ rárá.
Wọ́n ní àwọn ó kọ ohungbogbo sílè,
Àwọn ó máa sáré mọ́ owó.
Ọ̀rúnmìlà ní eyítí ẹ ńro níti owó bẹ́ẹ̀ni.
Àti eyítí e ńro níti owó bẹ́ẹ̀kó sì.
Ifá l'á bá máa yẹ́.
Ọgbọ́n l'á bá má yé.
Àwọn l'á bá bu iyìn fún.
Agbéniga l'àá pé owó; abìwàjé l'àá pé owó.
Enití bá fẹ́ràn owó l'áféjú, íwà rẹ̀ á bàjé.
Ìwà rere ni ọ̀sọ́ ènìyàn.
Bí ẹ ní owó l'ọ́wọ kò wípé kí ẹ má di afójú.
Kò wípé kí ẹ́ má di aṣiwèrè.
Kò wípé kí ẹ́ má di arọ.

82:1

Kò wípé kí ẹ má di olókúnrún àti bẹ̀ẹ̀bẹ̀ẹ̀.
Àbùkù ara gbogbo lè dé bá yín.
Ẹ jẹ́ lọ tún ọgbọ́n gbọ́n.
Kí ẹ tún èro gbà.
Kí ẹ mú ìwà rere.
Kí ẹ mú ọgbọ́n
Kí ẹ wá rúbọ
Kí ara lè rò nyin tinútòde.

86:1

One who does not build a house, does not
have to sleep in the tree top.
One who does not cultivate yams, does not
have to eat dirt off the ground.
And an adult who learns the teachings of Ifa,
does not have to eat old kola nuts.

Kò kọ́lé, kò sùn orí'gi
Kò kọṣu, kò jẹ erùpe ilẹ́
Àgbà kan kọ́ Ifá, kò jẹ obì gbó.

ÌWÒRÌ'ÒSÁ

87

87:1

Atikaresete, the self-adjuster, the priest of
heaven,
Interpreted the teachings of Ifa for Olodumare
and the world,
When the people of the world were running to
Olodumare for everything,
Crying out "Baba, Father, I have come.
Save me; please save me."
Olodumare said: "What is the matter?
Those whom I have given ability do not
use their ability.
And those whom I have given wisdom do not
use the wisdom I have given them."
It is said: children who do not see their parents,
Will strive for their own inner strength.

87: I

Atikareşetẹ, awo ọ̀run
A dífá fún Olódùmarè àti ayé
Nígbàtí àwọn ọmọ-aráyé ńsáre tọ̀
Olódùmarè nítorí ohun gbogbo
Ńké Baba, Baba, mo dé.
Gbà mi; jọ̀wọ́ gbà mi.
Olódùmarè ní: èétiri?
Ẹnití mo fún l'ágbára, kò lo agbára.
Ẹnití mo fún l'ógbọ́n, kò lo ọgbọ́n
wọn tí mo fún wọn.
Wọ́n ní àwọn ọmọ tí kò rí àwọn òbí wọn
Wọ́n màá sá ipá inú wọn.

ÌKÁ'WÒRÌ

90

90:1

The self-injurer; one who acts against himself.
One who throws ashes is followed by
those ashes.
One who does evil deeds injures himself in
equal measure.
This was the teaching of Ifa for Inukogun,
the one not-straight-inside,
Who was planning to do evil.
They said that the evil things that he was
going to do,
Would, in the end, return to ruin him.
They said that he should sacrifice,
And that he should give up his evil conduct.

ÌKÁ'WÒRÌ

90

90: 1

Ṣe'ra-rẹ̀; se ara rè.
Ẹnití ó dà eérú ni eérú itọ̀.
Ṣìkàṣìkà fi ìdájí sẹ'ra rẹ̀ .
A dífá fún Inúkògún,
Ńgbèrò ibi.
Wọ́n ní kí ohun burúkú tí ó máà se yìí,
Yóò dẹ̀hìn bọ̀wá bàjẹ́ òun.
A níkí ó wá rúbọ.
Kí ó kọ ìwà ìkà sílè.

ÌWÒRÌ ÒTÚRÁ
93

93:1

A crooked stick diffuses fire.
And a mad man scatters his own home.
This was the teaching of Ifa for Baba Ejo,
the father of snakes, and his children.
They said the children of a snake would never
be able to come together
So that they might offer effective resistance
on the day of battle.
They said if Baba Ejo, the father of snakes,
wanted them to come to agreement,
That they must sacrifice.
They heard, but they did not comply.

ÌWÒRÌ ÒTÚRÁ

93

93:1

Igi wóróko̩ níí tú iná ká.
Asiwèrè níí tú ilé ara rè̩ ká.
A dífá fún Baba Ejò àti o̩mo̩ rè̩.
Wó̩n ní: àwo̩n o̩mo̩ ejò kò̩ ní lé
        ni àjo̩hun kí wó̩n kó ara wo̩n jo̩,
Kí wo̩n kò̩yà l'ó̩jó̩ ìjà.
Wó̩n ní bí Baba Ejò bá pé kí wó̩n ni àjo̩hun
Kí wó̩n wá rúbo̩.
Wó̩n gbó̩; wó̩n kò rúbo̩.

94:1

Even in the adversity of famine, we must not eat hot stew hastily.
For if we eat hot stew hastily,
It will surely burn our mouths.
This was the teaching of Ifa for Akinsuyi.
They said: the year of prosperity is coming,
And that he should not act thoughtlessly.
They said he should sacrifice.
He heard and practiced sacrifice.

K'á má fi'pọ́njú ìyàn lá ọbẹ̀ gbígbóná.
Bí a bá fi'pọ́njú ìyàn lá ọbẹ̀ gbígbóná,
Dájúdájú a máà jó'ni l'ẹnú.
A dífá fún Akínsuyì.
Wọ́n ní: ọdún ọrọ̀ dé,
Àti kí ó má ṣe láìrónú.
Wọ́n ní: kí ó rúbọ.
Ó gbọ́; ó rúbọ

95

95:1

Nurture them gently; cultivate them carefully,
So that the people of the world might
not go wrong.
Anyone who does good, does it for herself.
And anyone who does evil, does it to herself.
This was the teaching of Ifa interpreted
for the world.
They said thieves should refrain from stealing.
They said anyone who steals a thousand things
from people will lose two thousand
things in life.
Anyone who sees a person in need should show
him kindness.
And anyone who does a thousand good deeds
will receive two thousand in return.
Surely, Oluwa, our Lord will reward him.

95:1

Arọratẹ̀ wọ́n; rọra tẹ̀ wọ́n.
Kí àwọn ọmọ-arayé má ṣìwafu.
Ẹnití ṣe rere, ó ṣeé fún ara rẹ̀.
Ẹnití ṣe ìkà, ó ṣeé fún ara rẹ̀.
Ni Ifá tí a dá fáyé.
Wọ́n ní àwọn olè kí wọ́n yé jàlè mọ́.
Wọ́n ní enití jí wọn l'ẹgbẹ̀rún,
a ṣòfo ẹgbàwá l'ayé.
Ẹnití rí akẹ́bọje kí ó fi oore ṣee.
Ẹnití ṣ'oore ẹgbẹ̀rún, a fi gb'ẹgbàwá.
Dandan, Oluwa wa ló máa san án.

ÌRẸTẸ̀'WÒRÌ
96

96: 1

One who has to eat corn meal without
condiments complains that
it's wrapped in leaves.
And one who has to scrape food from
wrapping leaves,
Wonders what one should do.
This was the teaching of Ifa interpreted
for Otewori,
Who said that he was going to the forest to
hang himself *because of adversity*.
They said: Otewori, do not hang yourself yet.
They are bringing you the symbolic
leaves of rulership now.

96:1

A ṣọ́n ẹ̀kọ sùn ní t'òun pọ́n.
Ẹnití ó fá ewé orí,
Èwo ni k'ó se?
Ó dá fún Ọ̀tẹ̀wòrì
T'ó sọ wípé òun nre ìgbẹ́ rè'so.
Wọ́n ní: Ọ̀tẹ̀wòrì, má tìí so.
Wọ́n ńmu ewé ire oyè ńbọ̀.

96:2

War ruins the world.
And intrigue undermines the people.
This was the interpretation of the teachings
of Ifa for Olofin Iwatuka.
They said: Olofin, war is coming.
Therefore, if you want to be victorious,
You should practice sacrifice.
Olofin heard, but he did not comply.

Ogún bayé jẹ́.
Àti ọ̀tọ̀ ńte ọmọ ènìyàn rí.
A dáfá fún Ọlọ́fin Iwàtuka.
Wọ́n ní: ogun máa dé o, Ọlọ́fin
Nítorínáà bí Ọlọ́fin bá wípé kí òun ṣẹ́gun,
Kí ó rúbọ.
Ọlọ́fin gbọ́; kò rúbọ.

ÌWÒRÌ'ỌṢẸ̀
97

97:1

Adversity does not come without bringing
its good aspects to us.
That which is evil and that which is good
come together.
This was the teaching of Ifa for one called
"The-lack-of-money-disables-a-person."
They said: one who experiences adversity,
should not lose hope,
And that she should maintain her good name.
For the sweetness of the bitter eruwo leaf comes
after *its transformation through cooking*.
They said she should practice sacrifice,
So that adversity can likewise be turned into
prosperity for her.

97:1

Ìṣẹ́ kìí dé kí ó má mú ire rẹ̀ bọ̀'ni.
T'ibi t'ire èjì wápò.
A dífá fún"Owó-kòsí-ènìyàn-kò-sunwọ̀n."
Wọ́n ní: ojù tí ó rí ìṣẹ́, kí ó má bà'ra jẹ́,
Kí ó tọ́jú orúko rere rẹ̀.
Adún nii gbẹ̀hin ewúro.
Wọ́n níkí ó rúbọ,
Kí ìṣẹ́ lè di ọrọ̀ fún un sì.

ÒFÚN'WÒRÌ

100

100:1

If we are kind, the children of others
will become our children.
This was the teaching of Ifa for
Obonhunbonhun,
Who had built a house and accumulated
a lot of wealth,
But who had no children at all.

Bí a bá n'ínúrere, ọmọ ọlọ́mọ a máa
di ọmọ eni.
A dífá fún Obọ̀nhùnbọ̀hùn,
Ti ó kọ́lé àti kásẹ tán,
Ṣùgbọ́n tí kò bímo rárá.

104

104:1

Accept a thing of value and hold on to it.
Keep it safe.
And when we are asked for it,
We should give the thing to its owner.
Goodness lies in not keeping it for ourselves.
They said: May we see our ancestors,
And that anyone who returns things to
their owner
Will never be empty-handed.

Gba ohun iyè; dáníi.
Gbàa láìléwu.
Bí a bá bi ẹni
K'á fi ohun náà fún ọlọ̀hun
Ire ni àìgbá fún ara ẹni
Wọ́n ní: t'ó a bá rí wọn;
Ẹnití ńfi ohun fún ọlọ̀hun
Kò ma yéé ni lọ́wọ́.

104:2

Leave them alone.
Let them run.
It is their character which is continuously
chasing them around.
This was the teaching of Ifa for Aniwonikun,
the person of bad conscience,
Who was constantly afraid day and night.
They said: "you should cultivate your character;
You should conduct yourself well, Akinwonikun,
So that you might stop running around
like a coward."

Ẹ jò wọ́n.
Ẹ jẹ́ wọ́n sá.
Ìwà wọn ni máa lé wọn kiri.
A dífá fún Aníwọnìkùn
Tí yíò máa bẹ̀rù tọ̀sań tòru.
O jẹ́ hùwà re;
O jẹ́ hùwà àtàtà, Aníwọnìkùn,
Kí o yé sá kiri bí ojo.

ÌDÍ ÒGÚNDÁ

109

109:1

Orunmila said Ogun's house is empty.
I said Ogun's house is empty.
We arrived at Ogun's house and did not find anyone.
I asked why have we arrived at Ogun's house and found no one?
The whole house was completely empty.
They said: Ogun's character was not good.
Therefore, should we expect that Ogun's house would be crowded?

Ọ̀rúnmìlà ní ìdí Ògún dá.
Mo ní ìdí Ògún dá.
A délé Ògún a kò bẹ́nìkan.
Mo ní èétirí tí a dé ilé Ògún tí a kò bẹ́nìkan
Gbogbo ilé dá késekése.
Wọ́n ní: ìwà Ògún kò sunwọ̀n
Ǹjé bí a bí wípé kí ilé Ògún kún sómúsómú?

112:1

Orunmila said good news is thing of joy.
I say good news.
He said that you should come join us
and tell everyone
That the person we have been looking for
has indeed arrived.

Ọ̀rúnmìlà ní àgbọ́ká òràn ayọ̀.
Èmi ní àgbóká.
Ó níkí ẹ wá bá wa wí fún gbogbo ènìyàn
Ẹnití a ńwà mà dé o.

ÒTÚRÚPỌ̀N'DÍ

116

116:1

The world is nice, but heaven is truly good.
Odudua said the people of the world
should return to heaven,
So that they might be reincarnated.
The young people said they would not go.
The elders also said they would not go.
We asked why?
They said: heaven does not readily let
return those who would go.
Orunmila said "heaven is beautiful.
It is the home of beauty.
Odudua would not live in a place which
is not good.
It is in a good place we find the orisha.
One who is called should answer the call.
A mother does not call her child to come
and suffer."

116:1

But the people were still reluctant
It was said that they should sacrifice
So that the darkness might be lifted and
removed from their eyes,
And so that when they are worried,
They would be able to look up to heaven.
But they did not sacrifice.

116:1

Ilé ayé dára; ọ̀run ma sunwọ̀n, o.
Odùduwà níkí àwọn ọmọ aráyé màá padà wá
Kí òun máa tún wọn se.
Ọmọdé ní òun kò lọ.
Àgbàlagbà ní òun kò lọ.
A ní èétirí?
Wọ́n ní: ọ̀run kò yá rébọ àwọn ìbá máa lọ.
Ọ̀rúnmìlà ní: ọ̀run dára
Ọ̀run ni ilé ẹwà.
Odùduwà kò jẹ́ gbé ibi tí kò sunwọ̀n.
Ibi rere ni a íbá òrìṣà
Ẹnití a bá pè kí ó jẹ́ ìpè.
Abiamo kí ipe ọmọ wá joró
Síbèsíbè ọmọ aráyé ńkọ̀dí.
A níkí wọ́n rúbọ
Kí òkùnkún lè ká kúrò lójú wọn.
Bí wọ́n ńṣíṣé kí wọ́n lè máa wò ọ̀run.
Wọ́n kọ̀ rúbọ.

ÌDÍ ÌRẸTẸ̀

119

119:1

It is gentle character which enables the
rope of life to remain strong
in our hands.
This was the teaching of Ifa for Orunmila,
Who was going to use gentle character
To obtain the rope of life from the
four hundred and one divine powers.

Ìwà pẹ̀lẹ́ fi okùn ayé rọ́ pẹ́tí lọ́wọ́ ẹni.
Ó dá fún Ọ̀rúnmìlà,
Tí ó ńlọ fi ìwà pẹ̀lẹ́
Gba okún ayé lówó ọ̀kan-lé-ní-rín wó ìmàlẹ̀.

119:2

Ijimere, the babalawo of physical fitness
and surpassing beauty,
Interpreted the teachings of Ifa for the
one who sees what is to be done and
does not do it; the irresponsible
comfort seeker.
They said one should sacrifice so that work
might appeal to one who fears it.
The *symbols* of the sacrifice: a hoe, a sword,
a dog and a ram.
We asked why?
Ifa said:
A hoe never refuses to work.
A sword never becomes sick.
A dog uses his head to fight through the forest
to come to work.
And a ram does not fear struggle.

119:2

Ìjímère, awo ìdárayá asunwọ̀n lẹ́wà
Ló dífá fún Aríṣemáṣe Ìdíręt̀èrẹtẹ̀
Wọ́n níkí ó wá ṣ'ẹbọ kí iṣẹ́ lè máa wu
ní ṣe ẹni ẹ̀rù iṣẹ́ ńbà.
Ẹbọ: ọkọ́, àdá, ajá àti àgbò
A ní èétirí?
Ifá ní:
Ọkọ́ kìí ko iṣẹ́ sílè.
Àdá kíí ṣ'òkùnrùn.
Ajá ńforí já igbò wá ṣiṣé.
Ẹ̀rù ìjà kìí bàgbò.

119:3

He who repays good and evil will
certainly repay.
He will not fail to repay.
He who questions will certainly question.
He will not fail to question.
This is the teaching of Ifa given to Orunmila,
Who, in turn, gave admonition to the people
Male and female.

Ẹlẹ́san á sán ire àti ibi.
Kà ṣàì sán.
Abèèrè á bèèrè
Kà ṣàì bèèrè.
Ó dá fún Ọ̀rúnmìlà,
T'ó ṣe kìlọ̀kìlọ̀ fún ènìyàn,
Tako tabo.

122:1

We should not catch a thief and then not
subdue him.
If we overcome him, we should constrain
the offender.
For if we do not constrain the offender,
That person whom we defeated,
when he has finished resting,
Will claim he defeated us.
This was the teaching of Ifa for Saanuote,
one who is overly lenient
with offenders.
He was asked to sacrifice so that his
excessive compassion would not
bring him to ruin.
The Lord of Heaven loves all things,
But he does not love them to an excess.

122:1

A kìí mólè kí á má yán an.
Bí a bá ṣẹ́gún, kí á mọ́lọ̀tẹ́ dè.
Bí a kò mọ́lọ̀tẹ́ dè,
Ẹnití a ṣẹ́, bí ó bá simi tán,
Á ní òun ni ó ṣẹ́ni.
A dífá fún Sàánú-ọ̀tè
A níkí ó wá rúbọ kí àṣejù àánú
má baà sọọ di abòṣì.
Ohun gbogbo ni Ọlọ́run fẹ́,
Ọlọ́run kò fẹ́ aṣejù.

122:1

ÀṢOYÉ

This is a teaching on the need for moderation in emotions, even positive ones like compassion and love. It is directed toward the *saanú-ọ̀tẹ̀*, literally the one-who-is lenient-with offenders, that is to say, those who violate moral and legal rules of the community, who betray and conspire against the good. The teaching tells us that if we catch an offender, we must not simply let him or her go, but must constrain him or her. This implies the need not only to constrain in the physical or literal sense of the word *dè* which is used here and means tie, bind, hobble, fetter, etc. It also implies the need to discipline offenders in such a way that they not benefit from their offense, so that they recognize its wrongness and so that they not be left with the illusion that they got away with their wrong-doing or even, as the texts say, are able to claim they defeated us.

This teaching tells us that excessive compassion and leniency toward wrong-doing, *àṣejù aanú*, can bring us to ruin. The implication here is that excess, even in positive emotions, leaves us vulnerable to misuse, injury and ruin. The teaching further suggests that we should follow the divine example of the Lord of Heaven, who is compassionate and loving toward all things--human, natural and spiritual, but *not* to an excess.

124:1

You cause trouble, but you don't
ask forgiveness.
You don't ask for forgiveness
You offer indignant denials,
making a lot out of little things.
This was the teaching of Ifa for Shakeu,
the offspring of Ibagboloro
On the day he was going to take the
stone of rulership to the moutain
as part of his coronation.
They said he should sacrifice so that no one would
threaten him in his bid for the throne.
But Shakeu refused to sacrifice,
For he was the son of a king and possessed
much wealth.
When the king died, Shakeu asked:
Who now is there in this world for me to
compete with for this title?
He dared to go to heaven *to compete*.

ÒFÚN'DI
124

124:1

He stretched out a rope to climb the moutain
toward heaven.
The Lord of Heaven spoke and asked Shakeu:
"Did you not find anyone in all the earth with
whom you could compete?"
He told Shakeu that he must never do
anything like this again.
When Shakeu was returning to earth,
Eshu cut the rope he used to climb the
mountain toward heaven.
He cut it at the top and the bottom,
And Shakeu was left hanging in mid-air.
Ifa says the Lord of Heaven wants to give
the lamp of destiny to someone,
But this person should be careful so that
he is not over ambitious and ruin it;
So that he, himself, does not break the rope
and block the way *to prosperity*.

124:1

O ṣe ọ̀ràn, o kò bẹ̀bẹ̀.
Ìwọ kò bẹ̀bẹ̀ ọ̀ràn.
Ìwo nṣe oníkojú yánràn yánràn.
A dífá fún Ṣakeu ti iṣe ọmọ Ìbagboloro,
Níjó tí ó nlọ mú ota oyè lóke
Wọ́n níkí ó rúbọ kí aráyé má bá dá níjì.
Ṣakeu kò rúbọ.
Ṣakeu jẹ́ ọmọ ọba ó sì là púpò.
Nígbàtí ọba kú, Ṣakeu ní:
"Tani òun tún lè dù oyè ḍé ọ̀dọ̀rẹ̀ mọ́
nínú ayé yìí."
Nígbànáà, ó gbọ́dọ̀ lọ sí ọ̀run.
Ó ta okùn gùn òkè lọ sí ọrun
Ọlọ́run ni, ó bèèrè Ṣakeu:
"Ìwọ, kò rí enití ìwọ yió dù oyè l'ọ́dọ̀
ni gbogbo ayé mọ́?"

124:1

Ó níkí ó má sẹ báyìí mọ́.
Nígbàtí Ṣakeu ńpadà bọ̀ wá sí ayé,
Okún tí ó fi gùn òkè lọ sí ọrun Ẹsù já.
Ó jáa l'óri nísàlẹ̀.
Ṣakeu wà dúró sí agbedeméjì ọ̀run.
Ifá ní Ọlọ́run fẹ́ gbé àtùpà ìwà fún ẹníkan
Kí ó ṣọ́ra kí ó mà bà fi àsejù bàjẹ́
Kí ó má bá já okùn di ojú.

124:2

The teachings of Ifa were interpreted
for Olori Oga.
They said that anyone who restricts
goodness to the house,
Will never obtain goodness on the outside.
They said she should sacrifice,
So that goodness might flow into the house.

A dífá f'Olorì Ògá.
Wọ̀n níkí ẹnití ó dí ire mọ'lé,
Kí rí t'òde gbà.
Wọ̀n níkí ó wá rúbọ,
Kí ire báa lè ṣan wá ilé.

127:1

If we practiced the principle "share with
me that I may share with you,"
The world would be an orderly place.
This was the teaching of Ifa for Orunmila,
Who was going to Otu-Ife
To teach the people the rules of conduct
at home and the rules of conduct
in the countryside.

Bùfúnmi kí mibùfún o
Ayé a máa gún.
A dífá f Ọ̀rúnmìlà,
Ti ó ńlọ s'Otù-Ìfè
Kọ́ wọn ní ìṣe ilé àti ìṣe oko.

129:1

A leader does not send insults
A leader wards off insults.
Anyone who cannot ward off insults,
Will continue to suffer from them.
This was the teaching of Ifa for Ologbo,
the son of a babalawo.
Ologbo said that he would triumph over
all opposition,
And that he would see the end of his enemies.
He was advised to sacrifice.
He heard and complied.

129:1

Olú kò ńrán ìwòsì;
Olú kòyà ìwòsí.
Ẹnití kò lè kòyà ìwòsì,
Ìyà kìí yé wọn íjẹ.
A dífa f'Ọlọ́gbo ọmọ awo.
Ọlọ́gbo ni òun máa ṣègún gbogbo òdí,
Àti òun máa rí ẹ̀hìn ọ̀tá.
A níkí ó wá rúbọ.
Ó gbọ́; ó rúbọ.

Òkànràn'Rosú

130

130:1

Knowingly doing evil is not good.
If a person who does evil apologizes,
The matter will be resolved.
Everyone forgives those who do wrong
unknowingly.
This was the teaching of Ifa for the
one who confronts matters,
the courageous one, Mebelufe
Whose name means "I will not beg
even the king."
Everyone was continually complaining
about him.
If he would just apologize, people would
say the matter is finished.
Then, one day it happened.

ÒKÀNRÀN'ROSÚ

130

130:1

Ìmọ̀ọ́mọ̀ ṣe ibi kò sunwọ̀n.
Ẹnití ńṣe ibi, bí o bá bẹ̀bẹ̀ ọ̀ràn,
Ọ̀ràn á tán.
Gbogbo ayé ní ńfi orí jì àìmọ̀
A dífá fún oṣọ̀ràn, kin, Mẹbẹlufe
Gbogbo wọ́n ni ńfi ẹjọ́ rẹ̀ sùn.
Bí ó bá bẹ̀bẹ̀ ọ̀ràn,wọ́n á ní: ó tán
Ó wá di níjọ̀kan.

131:1

Olorun, the Lord of Heaven does not
demand sacrifice.
Nor does he request material things.
But anyone who seeks the good will
practice sacrifice.
For it is Olorun, the Lord of Heaven, who says
that humans should sacrifice.

Ọlọ́run kò tọrọ ẹbọ.
Béeni ko bèèrè erú.
Ṣùgbọ́n ẹnití wá ire níí ṣẹbọ
Ọlọ́run; ó wípé kí àwọn ọmọ-arayé máà ṣẹbọ.

131:2

Today, we say "Orunmila,"
This means that "The Lord of Heaven
is the one who owns real riches."
It is He who can give to anyone according
to his will.

Lóòní a wípé: Ọrúnmìlà
Ìtúmọ̀ èdè yi nipé Ọlọ́run níkan ló
ní ọlá lọ́wọ́.
Òun sì lè fún ẹnikẹ́ni gẹ́gẹ́bí ó ti wù ú.

135:1

The sound of a bell is heard far and wide.
This was the teaching of Ifa for Orunmila.
They said that in every place around the world
People would hear his name,
And that they would seek to know him.
They said he should sacrifice,
So that he would be at peace.
He heard and complied.

Ìró agogo àgbọ́ká.
A dífá f'Ọ̀rúnmìlà.
Wọ́n ní níbí gbogbo ayíká ayé
Ni wọ́n ma gbọ́ orúko rẹ̀.,
Tí wọ́n sì máa wà mọ̀ọ́.
Wọ́n níkí ó rúbọ.
Kí ara lè rọ̀ọ́.
Ó gbọ́; ó rúbọ.

ÒTÚRÁ-IROSU

140

140:1

Gently, Gently.
This was the advice of Ifa
For those at an impasse.
They said that they should sacrifice
So that all they were doing would not
 come to an impasse.
But those at the impasse did not sacrifice.
So, they tried to get money but it did not work.
They tried to have children but it was
 not successful.
They tried to get wives and husbands but
 it came to naught also.
Everything they were doing came to an impasse.
Ifa says a person should practice sacrifice
So that he will not encounter an impasse in
 what he does,
And so that things will not slip from her grasp,
And she be unable to hold on to anything.

ÒTÚRÁ-IROSU

140

140:1

Wúyẹ́wúyẹ́.
A dífá fún wón ní tibọ́.
Wọ́n níkí wọ́n rúbọ,
Kí ohun gbogbo tí wọ́n máa ṣe
Kí ó má bá máa ṣe tibọ́.
Wón kò rúbọ ní tibọ́.
Báyìí wọn ṣe ọ̀ràn owó, ó di tibọ́.
Wón ṣe ọ̀ran ọmọ, ó di tibọ́.
Wón sì ṣe ọ̀ràn aya àti ọkọ, ó di tibo pẹ̀lú.
Ohun gbogbo ti wọ́n ńṣe ni, ó nbọ̀ sí tibọ́.
Ifá ní kí ẹníkan rúbọ,
Kí ó má bá máa rí òràn tibọ́.
Kí ohun ti ó múu má bọ́ lọ́wọ́ rẹ̀,
Kò sì lè tẹ̀ ni ohunkóhun.

ÒFÚN'ROSÚ

146

146:1

Ofun is giving out goodness everywhere.
Ofun does not make noise about it.
People like this are difficult to find in the world.
Anyone who wants to do wonderful things
should observe the ways of heaven.
Heaven is the home of honor.
This was the teaching of Ifa for humans.
It was said that death would bring them
to see the ways of heaven
They were asked to sacrifice,
So that there would be no darkness and
grief on their way.
They heard but they did not sacrifice.

146:1

Òfún ńfún ire ká.
Òfún kò pariwo.
Ènìyàn bí irú wọ̀nyí ṣọ̀wọ̀n layè.
Ẹni máà dáṣà kí ó wò ìṣe ọ̀run.
Ọ̀run nilé ọlá.
A dífá f'àwọn ènìyàn.
A ní ìkú a máa mú wọ́n lọ fún àwọn wò ìṣe ọ̀run
A níkí wọ́n rúbọ
Kí ó má báa sí òkúnkún àti ìbànújé lọ́nà wọn.
Wọ́n gbọ́; wọ́n kò rúbọ.

147:1

She sees me. I don't see her.
This was the teaching of Ifa for Owa.
They said that which we are looking for
is near us,
But we do not recognize it.
Orunmila, Witness to Destiny, said:
The very thing we are looking for is near us,
But our lack of knowledge prevents our
seeing it.

Ó rí mi. N kò ríi.
A dífá fún Ọwa.
Wọn ní: ohun tí à ńwá ńbẹ nítòsí ẹni.
Àfi àìmọ̀ ẹni.
Ọ̀rúnmìlà, Ẹlẹ́rí Ìpín, ó ní:
Ohun tí a ńwá ńbe nítòsí ẹni.
Àfi àìmọ̀ ẹni ni kìí jẹ́ ká ríi.

149

149:1

One day is a day of laughter.
Another day is a day of crying.
This was the teaching of Ifa for Egasheshe,
the bird on the cotton tree.
He asked: "which is this one?"
They said: "a day of joy and a day of amusement."
He was advised to sacrifice.
He heard and complied.

Ọjọ́ kan ńbẹ ọjọ́ èrín.
Ọjo míràn ńbẹ ojó ẹkún.
A dífá fún Egaṣẹṣẹ ẹyẹ orí òwú
Ò ní: èwo li èyí?
Wọ́n ní: ọjọ́ ayọ̀ àti ọjọ́ eré.
A níkí ó rúbọ.
Ó gbọ́; ó rúbọ.

149:2

One day is a day of laughter.
Another day is a day of crying.
We asked: "which day will this one be?"
They said: "a day of sorrow."
This was the teaching of Ifa for
Obahun Ijapa,
Who treated matters as if weeping
were laughter.
They said: "today is a day of
false accusations,"
And therefore, he should sacrifice.
He heard, but he would not sacrifice.
He said there was no matter on
earth that could affect him,
That he could not laugh about.
But he finally sacrificed when the
false accusations became too
much for him.

149:2

Ọjọ́ kan ńbẹọjọ́ ẹ̀rín.
Ọjọ́ míràn ńbẹ ọjọ́ ekún.
A ní: èwo ni a kàn yí?
Wọ́n ní:ọjọ́ ìbànújé.
A dífá f'Ọbahun Ìjàpá
A fọ̀ràn bí ekún s'ẹ̀rín.
Wọ́n ní: loní ọjọ́ ẹdúnrúnmọ́
Nítorí náà kí ó rúbọ.
Ó gbọ́ ; kò rúbọ.
Ó ní: kòsí ọ̀ràn ìbànújé lè kàn
    òun láyé.
Kí òun má fi ṣe ẹ̀rín rín.
Ó wá rúbo níkẹhìn nígbàtí
    ẹdúnrúnmọ́ pàpọ̀jù.

150:1

Be able to suffer without surrendering;
persevere in what you do.
This was the teaching of Ifa for Okanran
They said: A case has come, but it is the one
who ridicules us who will suffer.
They said that sacrifice should be made
So that Okanran might not die dealing
with the case
He heard and he sacrificed.
They said that Okanran will surely get
some rest.
Pigeons gather good things on the right and
on the left to bring into the house.
Long is the lifetime of a sheep.
She has been given this blessing,
So that she might have the opportunity to
enjoy her life.

150:1

Rọ́jú. Forítìí
A dífá Ọ̀kànràn.
Wọ́n ní: ejọ́ de ti a f'ni rẹ́rìín lójú.
Wọ́n ní ẹbọ ni ká ṣe.
Kí Ọ̀kànràn máa kú ṣejọ́.
Ó gbọ́; ó rúbọ
Wọ́n ní Ọ̀kànràn á simi o.
Ọ̀tún àti òsì ni ẹyẹlé fi nko ire wọlé.
Ìgbà gígùn nítí àgútàn.
Agútàn ti gbà oore náà
K'a rójú ṣayé.

150:2

Letting people practice cruelty supports the
cruel person.
Allowing people to do evil sustains the
evil person.
This was the teaching of Ifa for those who
would not listen,
Who said that Orunmila was giving too many
warnings about wrongdoing,
And that they would do what they wanted.
They were doing evil.
They were committing acts of cruelty.
And things in life were going well for them.
People went to report this to Orunmila.
Orunmila said that regardless of how long it
may be, the one who rewards and
punishes will come around again
and again.

150:2

He will relieve people of their burdens in the end.
He will go about his work quietly.
And when he comes, all of them will run.
They said we should sacrifice
So that permissiveness towards cruelty and
allowance of evil,
Might not get an opportunity to become
a part of us;
And so that our companions and peers
might not deride and show contempt
for us in the end.

150:2

"Jẹ̀kó ṣekà" ńgbe oṣìkà.
"Jẹ̀kó ṣekà" ńgbe asẹbi.
A dífá f'awọn àfòìgbò
Tí wípé Ọ̀rúnmìlà nkìlò ọ̀ràn ju,
Ti inú àwọn li àwọn máa ṣe.
Wọ́n ńṣe ibi.
Wọ́n ńṣe ika.
Ohun ayé ńdára fún wọn.
A lọ wí fún Ọ̀rúnmìlà
Ọ̀rúnmìlà ni: bóbápẹ́tító, ẹlẹ́san
ńbòwá àyíká gbirigbiri.
Ó túmọ̀ l'ẹrù kálẹ̀.
A ṣe jẹ́jẹ́ ṣiṣé.
Bí ó bá dé, gbogbo wọn a sá.
Wọ́n níkí a ṣẹbọ kí "Jẹ̀kó ṣekà" àti
"Jékó ṣe'bi"
Má lè ráyè bọ́sì ikùn ẹni,
Kí àwọn ẹgbẹ́ àti ọ̀gbá má bá fi wá rẹ́rin
ẹlẹ́yà ni ìgbẹ̀hìn.

ÒGÚNDÁ WỌ̀NRÍN

152

152:1

The lazy person sleeps while the worker works.
And when the worker finishes his work,
Others begin to envy him.
This was the teaching of Ifa for Ogun.
They said that Ogun should sacrifice
So that those who were envying him
might be defeated.
He heard and sacrificed.
They said that calabash that makes an enemy
of the water jar
Will break on the way to the river.
And those who make an enemy of you
will be defeated also.

152:1

Ọ̀le ńsùn nígbàtí òṣìṣẹ́ ńṣiṣẹ́.
Òṣìṣẹ́ ṣeé tán,
Wọ́n ńṣe ìlàra.
A dífá f'Ogún
A níkí Ogún wá rúbọ
Kí àwọn ti ńṣe ìlàra rẹ̀ báa lè ṣẹ́gún.
Ó gbọ́; ó rúbọ.
Wọ́n ní: kèrègbe tí ó báa à mu ńṣe òtá
ọ̀na odò níí fọ́ si
Àwọn tí nba ó ṣe òtá yóò sì ṣẹ́gún.

152:2

May the battle I fight always add to my honor.
The battle that brings honor belongs
to the lion.
The battle that brings honor belongs to Aara.
Ogunda. You defeated them in struggle
everyday and everywhere.
May the battle I fight always add to my honor,
The battle that brings honor.

Ìjà tí n ó jà yí kími níyì sií.
Àjàgbuyì níti kìnìún.
Àjàgbuyì níti Àárá.
Ògúndá. Ìwọ ló ńdá wọn ni'jàkádì
lọ́jọ́ gbogbo nílẹ̀kílẹ̀
Ìjà tí n ó jà yí kími níyì sií.
Àjàgbuyì.

153:1

Elegbara does not run on the day of battle.
A battle of honor belongs to Elegbara.
Aara does not run on the day of battle,
And a battle of honor belongs to Aara.
The lion does not run on the day of battle,
And a battle of honor belongs to the lion.
I will not run on the day of battle,
And may my fellow soldiers not run
on the day of battle either.

Ẹlẹ́gbárá kìísá lọ́jọ́ ijà.
Àjàgbuyì níti Ẹlẹ́gbárá.
Ààrà kìísá lọ́jọ́ ijà.
Àjàgbuyì níti Ààrà.
Kìnìún kìísá lọ́jọ́ ijà.
Àjàgbuyì níti kìnìún.
Èmi kò máa sá lọ́jọ́ ijà.
Kí àwọn ọmọ ogun ẹ̀hìn mi má sàá lọ́jọ́ ìjà.

154:1

Ewe Omo interpreted the teachings of Ifa
for Osa.
They said: regardless of whether he runs
around in circles or not,
The world will still see him.
And they will ridicule him.
They said he should practice sacrifice,
So that matters of shame might not reach him.
He heard and complied.
After he had sacrificed, he heard the babalawo
chanting this Ifa chant:
"Indeed, Osa does not steal.
Indeed, Osa does not use evil potions.
Indeed, Osa does not reveal the secrets
of friends.
Indeed, Osa does not lie.
His affairs have become worthy of respect."
And all the people there joined in this chant.

154:1

Ewé Ọmọ li ó dífá f'Ọsá.
Wọ́n ní làíkàsí sísá ti ó má sá yí,
Ayé a ríí mú.
Wọ́n a máa fi rẹrìín.
Wọ́n ni ẹbọ níkí ó ṣe,
Kí ọ̀ran ìtíjú má báa dé síí.
Ó gbọ́; ó rúbọ.
Nígbàtí ó rúbo tán, à ńgbọ́ babaláwo
ńkorin orin Ifá yìí:
Ọ̀sá má máa jalè o hẹn!
Ọ̀sá má máa sa òògùn ìkà o, hẹn!
Ọ̀sá má máa tú àsírí ọ̀rẹ́ o, hẹn!
Ọ̀sá má máa ṣ'èké o, hẹn!
Ọ̀ràn rẹ̀ dayẹyẹ.
Gbogbo ènìyàn tí ó wà níbẹ̀
sì nbá wọ́n gbé orin náà.

155:1

I asked why is Owon laughing so lively?
Orunmila responded saying:
Owon is laughing so lively because:
There is money in the house;
There is a wife in the house;
There are children in the house.
Every good thing is in the house.
Indeed, Owon's life is exactly right.
Owon weighs everything in the balance.
Owon does not eat without measuring what he eats.
Owon does not drink without measuring what he drinks.
Owon does not use cloth without measuring what he uses.
And Owon does not build a house before making measurements of what he is going to build.

Ọ̀WỌ́NRÍN'KÁ
155

155:1

This was the teaching of Ifa for the Measurer-
of-all-Things at Ife-Ooye and
for the stranger.
They were asked to sacrifice so that they
would never lose balance.
They sacrificed; they were given Ifa leaves and
they accepted them.
It was said: What pincers hold firmly
does not fall.
And a bat does not hold on to a tree in
order to fall down.

ÒWÓNRÍN'KÁ
155

155:1

Mo ní eetirí ti Ọ̀wọ́n fi ńrín kààkàá?
Ọ̀rúnmìlà dáhùn ó ní: Ọ̀wọ́n nrín kààkàá nítorí:
Owó wà nílé;
Ayá wà nílé;
Ọmọ́ wà nílé.
Ohun rere gbogbo nílé.
Gan, ayé Ọ̀wọ́n gún gẹ́gẹ́.
Ọ̀wọ́n ngbé ohun gbogbo wà sórí ìwòn.
Ọ̀wọ́n kìí jeun kí ó má wọ̀n ọ́n kí ó tó jẹ́ẹ̀
Ọ̀wọ́n kìí mu kí ó má wọ̀n ọ́n kí ó tó muú.
Ọ̀wọ́n kìí lo aṣọ kí ó ma wọ́n kí ó tó lòó.
Ọ̀wọ́n kìí kọ́lẹ̀ kí ó ma wọ́n kí ó tó kọ́ọ.
A dífá fún Afiwọ̀n-ṣe-ohun-gbogbo n'Ífẹ̀ Oòyè;
a bù fún àlejò.

155:1

A níkí wọ́n rúbọ kí wọn ma báa ju ìwòn
nù láìláì.
Wọ́n rúbọ; a ṣ'ewé Ifá fún wọn; wọ́n gbàa
A ní: ohun ẹ̀mú bá mú nídúróṣansan kìí bọ́.
Àdán kìí mú igi kí ó bọ́.

155:2

May we go away and may we come
back home.
If a child does not move around, the child
will not be wise.
This was the teaching of Ifa for Ademoorin
Ayankale, she who has learned to
walk and strolls around the house easily.
They said she should sacrifice
So that she might not fall into the hands
of death,
And if she fell into the hands of death,
That death would not be able to kill her.
She heard and sacrificed.

155:2

K'á rín lọ; k'á rín bọ̀wálé.
Bí ọmọ kò rìn, ọmo náà kìí gbọ́n.
Ni a dá f'Ademọ̀ọrín Ayankálé.
Wọ́n níkí wá rúbọ,
Kí ó má baà bọ́ s'ọwọ́ ikú,
Àti bí ó bá bọ́ s'ọwọ́ ikú,
Kí ikú má lè pa á.
Ó gbọ́; ó rúbọ.

155:3

Scarcity travels around the world.
This was the teaching of Ifa for Orunmila.
It was said that he should sacrifice
When he was travelling around this world,
So that the hands of detractors would not
touch and taint him.
He heard and complied.
They said that the fingernails of a person do not
infect kola nuts by carrying them.
They do not contaminate bitter kola
nuts by carrying them.
And they do not affect a joyful person.
Thus, may the hand of the detractors not be
able to touch and taint you either.

155:3

Ọ̀wọ́n rìn káyé.
A dífá fún Ọ̀rúnmìlà.
A níkí Ọ̀rúnmìlà à rúbọ
Bí òun ti máa ńrín ká ayé yìí,
Ki ọwọ́ àwọn abatẹnijẹ́ má lè ràn.
Ó gbọ́; ó rúbọ.
Wọ́n ni èékánná eléèkánná kìírán obì gbígbẹ
Èékánná eléèkánná kìírán orogbó gbígbè.
Èékánná eléèkánná kìírán ọmọ ayọ̀.
Ki owọ́ àwọn abatẹnijẹ́ kí ó maa lè ràn ọ.

156:1

The wicked do not weigh their conduct
before they act.
This was the teaching of Ifa given to Alabamo,
the one who regrets afterwards.
They said he should practice sacrifice,
So that he might do good things continuously.
He heard but he did not sacrifice.

Ìkà ènìyàn kìí wọ̀n ohun tirẹ̀ kí ó tóó ṣeé.
A dáa fún Alabààmọ̀.
Wọ́n níkí wá rúbọ.
Kí ó lè máa ṣe ohun rere.
Ó gbo ṣùgbọ́n kò rú.

156:2

Evil was whirling all around them,
But Owon was laughing.
This was the teaching of Ifa for the people at Ife Ooye.
They were advised to sacrifice
So that their enemies would not be able to remove them from their positions,
And so that their adversaries would not be able to detract from their honor.
They heard and they sacrificed.
The babalawo said: anyone who says that Ife should not expand in the world
Will be destroyed in the world.
We do not say that Ife should not expand in the world.
May we live long.
And may the mark we leave not be wiped out in the world.

156:2

Ìkà ńpòòyì ńyíká wọn.
Ọ̀wọ́n ńrérìín.
A dífá fún wọn ní Ifẹ̀-Oòyè.
A níkí wọ́n rúbọ.
Kí òtá má lè sí wọn nípo.
Kí òtá wọn má lè bù ọlá wọn kú.
Wọ́n gbọ́;wọ́n rú.
Babaláwo níi ẹnití ó bá wípé kí
Ifẹ́ má fẹ̀
A rún kùrò l'ayé.
Awa kò wípè kí Ifẹ́ má fẹ̀ o.
K'á s'ayé pẹ́
Kí ìlà tiwa má run nínú ayé.

Ọ̀WỌ́NRÍN OTÚRÀ
159

159:1

The constant soldier is never unready,
even once.
This was the teaching of Ifa for Igbin, the snail,
the courteous one.
Who was going to engage Ekun, the leopard
in a sudden fight.
They said that Ekun was always ready for battle,
And that Igbin should not engage him.
One whom we cannot engage in battle, we leave
to the Lord of Heaven.
They said he should sacrifice,
So that the lord of destiny might fight for him.
He understood and made the sacrifice.

159:1

Ìjàmájà kò túrasílẹ̀ lẹ́ẹ̀kan.
A dífá fún Ìgbín omẹ̀sọ̀,
Tí nlọ b'Ẹ̀kùn jìjà ọ̀jíjà.
Wọ́n ní: Ẹ̀kùn wà ni ìmúratẹ́lẹ́ nígbà gbogbo
Kí Ìgbín má ṣe
Ẹnití à kò lè mú, Ọlọ́run ni ààá fún.
Wọ́n níkí ó wá rúbọ.
Kí Ìpín lè jà fún un.
Ó gbọ́; ó rúbọ.

ÒTÚRÁ WỌ̀NRÍN
160

160:1

Travelers of earth and travelers of heaven,
we will see each other again.
Termites do not scatter without coming back
together again.
This was the teaching of Ifa for us humans
who were mourning the dead.
They said the place from which the people of
earth come is where they are returning.
What are the tears for then? Why the sorrow?
What is the raising oneself up and down for?
And why is there fasting?
He who sends us is he who calls us to
return home.
If a child does not know his father, the world
is not right.
It is death which takes the child so that he
may know heaven.
We will know darkness then.

Ọ̀TÚRÁ WỌ́NRÍN
160

160:1

Speak to me that I may speak to you.
It is by our voices we recognize each other
in the darkness.
If a child does not know her father, the world
is not right.
The people of the world were advised
to sacrifice.
They heard and they practiced sacrifice
So that they might live long on earth
And that they might experience goodness.

ÒTÚRÁ WỌ̀NRÍN
160

160:1

Èro ayé àt'èro ọ̀run, a ó tún'ra wa rí.
Ètútú kìí túká kí ó má gbárajọ.
A dífá f'àwa ènìyàn tíí máa sọkún òkú.
Wọ́n níkí ibi ọmọ-aráyé ti wá ni wọ́n ńpadà sí.
Èwo níti ẹkún? Èwo níti ìbànújẹ́?
Èwo níti igbaranṣalẹ? Èwo níti àìjẹun?
Ẹnití ó rán ni wá ló tún ńpẹni
padà kí a bọ̀wálé.
Ọmọ kò lè gba ìmọ̀ baba, k'áyé gún.
Ìkú l'ó mú ọmọ wá mọ̀ ọ̀run.
Awa ó mò òkùnkùn.
Fọ̀ sí mi kími fò sí ọ.
Òhun ni a fi ńmọ ara ẹni nínú òkùnkùn.
Ọmọ kò lè gba ìmọ̀ baba, k'áyé gún.
Wọ́n níkí ọmọ-aráyé rúbọ.
Wọ́n gbọ́;wọn rú nítorípé kí wọ́n
lè máa pẹ́ nínú ayé,
Àti pé kí wọ́n lè màa rí ire.

161:1

There is no war in the fields.
There is no intrigue in the cities.
This was the interpretation of Ifa
for Olofin Iwajo.
They said that the time of his rule
would be good.
They said that the Olofin should sacrifice
So that the joy of his reign would not cause
a lot of people to become lazy or
of unsound mind.
He heard and sacrificed.

Kòsí ogun ní pápá.
Kòsí ọ̀tẹ̀ lááarin ìlú.
A dífá fún Ọlọ́fin Iwajo.
Wọ́n ní: ọtẹ̀ rẹ̀ lórí oyé á sunwọ̀n.
Wọ́n níkí Ọlọ́fin rúbọ
Kí ayò igba rẹ̀ má lè mú òpọlọ́pọ̀
ènìyàn di ọ̀lẹ tàbí asínwin.
Ó gbọ́; ó rúbọ.

163

163:1

Owonrin does not do wrong.
Owonrin does not cause pain.
They are accusing Owonrin falsely.
It was said that Owonrin would triumph over them,
And that Owonrin should sacrifice
He heard and he complied.
And he placed the thunder stone on Ifa.

Ọ̀wọ́nrín kò sẹ̀.
Ọ̀wọ́nrín kò rò.
Wọ́n ńdùrùnmọ́ Ọ̀wọ́nrín.
A ní Ọ̀wọ́nrín á sẹ́gun wọn.
Kí Ọ̀wọ́nrín wá ṣ'ebo.
Ó gbọ́; ó rúbọ.
Ó fi ẹ̀dún-ààrá lé Ifá.

165:1

The teachings of Ifa were interpeted for the
people of Ife-Ooye.
They said a time is coming when the people
of earth
Will travel through the air of earth and heaven
like a bird.
They said that the city of Ife should
practice sacrifice,
So that it might not suffer numerous losses
at that time.
It would not begin at Ife, but would go
around the world.
The people heard but they did not sacrifice.
They said they had sacrificed to walk on earth;
They would not walk in the air.

165:1

A dífá fún wọn ní Ifẹ́-Oòyè.
Wọ́n ní: ìgbà kan nbọ̀wá ìgbàtí
àwọn ọmọ-aráyé
Yóo má rín ni òfuurufú ayé àti ọ̀run bí ẹyẹ.
Wọ́n níkí wọ́n nílú náà wá rúbọ
Kí ó má bá sì òfò púpò nígbànáà.
Kò ni bẹ̀rẹ̀ ní Ifẹ̀ ṣùgbọ́n òfò ti ó màá
múwá yóò kárí ayé
Wọ́n gbọ́; wọ́n kò rú.
Wọ́n ní àwọn ti rúbọ à tẹ̀pẹ́ lórí ilẹ̀;
Àwọn kò ni rín lòfuurúfú.

166:1

The teachings of Ifa were interpreted for Igun,
the vulture,
And likewise for Osin, the fish eagle,
On the day that those who take people away
were arriving from the heavens,
On the day that spirits from heaven
were appearing.
They said that Igun and Osin should sacrifice
So that they would not die an accidental death.
Osin refused to sacrifice.
He said that what the Lord of Heaven made,
He did not leave unfinished.
Igun said his future did not look promising
And that as for him, he was going to sacrifice.
So, he sacrificed.
Afterwards, the babalawo said:
That he should go forth without fear,
And that he should go forth with dignity and
measured movement.

166:1

A dífá fún Igún
A bu fún Ọsin,
Níjó tí múni-múni òrun dé,
Níjó tí ẹ̀mimọ ọ̀run ńhàn.
Wọ́n níkí Igún àti Ọsin rúbọ
Nítorí ikú à-sì-kú.
Ọsin kọ̀ kò rúbọ.
Ó ní ohun tí Ọlọ́run bá ti ṣe
Kí iṣe kù.
Igún ní orí rẹ̀ kò dára.
Ó ní oun yío rúbọ.
Ó rúbọ.
Nígbàtí Igún rúbọ tán,àwọn babaláwo ní
Kí ó lọ máa rín àìbèrù
Kí ó lọ máa yan.

166:2

Ofun, the Giving One, gives to them so that
they might nurture.
Ofun, the Giving One, gives to them so that
they might care for others.
This was the teaching of Ifa for Oduduwa
Who was doing good all over the world.
He said "doing good worldwide is the best
expression of character."
They said a part of the world would not thank
him for his kindness.
And others would not even recognize its value.
But he said "a father cannot help but give good
things to his children
And a mother cannot help but give good things
to her son or daughter."
They said that Orunmila should sacrifice
So that all the good things which he
gave to people,
If they were wasted in the world,
They would return to him in good order.
He heard and sacrificed.

166:2

Òfún fún wọn kẹ́.
Òfún fún wọn ṣọ́.
A dífá fún Odùduà
Ti ó máa ṣoore kárí ayé.
Ó níkí a soore kárí aye l'ó dárajù ni ìwà.
Wọ́n níkí apákan kò ní ṣọpẹ́ ooré lówó rẹ̀ .
Àwọn mìíràn kò tilẹ̀ ní mọ tiwon ílò.
Ṣùgbọ́n ó ní baba ọmọ kò lè ṣe kí ó
má fi ohun rere fún ọmọ.
Àti ìyá ọmọ kò lè ṣe kí ó má fi
ohun rere fún ọmọ.
Wọ́n níkí Odùduà wá rúbọ
Kí ohun rere gbogbo tí ó ńfi fún ènìyàn,
Bí wọ́n bá fi s'òfò ní ayé,
Kí wọ́n lè máà tún padà tó Odùduà l'ọ́wọ́.
Ó gbọ́; ó rúbọ.

167:1

Everyone in the world searches for
something good for themselves
Now, if mine would turn out well,
yours would turn out well also.
Everyone in the world searches for
something good for themselves.
It is another person who wishes bad things
for us.

Ggbogbo ayé ni ńwá ohun rere sí ara won.
Ǹjẹ́ tèmi ìbá dára, tìre ìbá dára.
Ggbogbo ayé ni ńwá ohun rere ti ara won.
Ẹni-ẹlẹ́ni ni iwá ohun burúkú fún-ni.

170:1

Tumultuous is the place of dancing.
Turbulent is the place of battle.
This was the teaching of Ifa for Ogun
When he was going to engage Obara in battle.
They said that Ogun would do well,
But that Ogun should practice sacrifice
So that Obara might not be killed in
the struggle.
He heard and sacrificed.
They said that a bird should not fight
another bird to the death.
And a basket of dry leaves is not heavy enough,
That its contents should kill someone.

170:1

Rìtìrìtì ni ojú ijó.
Rìtìrìtì ni ojú ìja.
A dífá fún Ògún
Ńlọ ba Òbàrà ja ìjà kan.
Wọ́n ní Ògún á dáa,
Ṣùgbọ́n kí Ògún wá ṣebọ
Kí Òbàrà má baà kú síi lọ́rùn.
Ó gbọ́; ó rú.
Wọ́n ní adìe kìí bá adìe jà kí ó kú.
Agbọ̀n ìràwé kìí wúwo
Kí ó d'éru pa'ni.

170:1

ÀSỌYÉ

This is a teaching on the need to respect and preserve human life. It begins by placing side by side the site of dancing and the site of battle, the place of sport and the place of fighting, the place of joy and the place of anger. And it notes that both places are rowdy or tumultuous and turbulent. The intention seems to be to suggest that things are likely to get out of hand in both contexts but that the person of character must hold to principle in both places. This is an important juxtaposition, because dancing is seen as more joyful and less serious than war, not a life and death matter. Thus, to place the site of dancing alongside the site of battle tends to suggest that claiming exoneration from extreme offences because the situation got out of hand is no more justifiable on the battlefield than it is on the dance floor.

The teaching is for Ogun, the divinity of war, iron and the human hardness and moral roughness this suggests. He is advised, concerning his battle with Obara, to sacrifice so that Obara might not be killed in the struggle. Now, a warrior makes war, a soldier does battle and they are trained to kill. But Ifa here tells the embodiment of the warrior, the divinity of war, to expect victory, do well in the struggle, but do not kill. He is asked to *sacrifice* so that Obara might not be killed in the struggle. Kawaida tradition reads this as a challenge to *sacrifice* self, not to give up one's life and lose the battle, but to sacrifice one's will to kill and cultivate the will to win without killing, to defeat without destroying.

This text and the Odu in general recognizes the constant need to struggle against opponents of varying degrees of opposition and evil. But what it says here is that humans should always fight in ways that show adequate respect for human life, beginning with each other. The analogy used here is that a bird should not fight another bird to the death. Furthermore, the text suggests that weighed against the heavy value of preserving human life, other issues are as light as a basket of dry leaves. And as the text says, "a basket of dry leaves is not heavy enough that its content should kill someone."

176:1

Honor goes forth from the house and
honor returns to the house.
This was the teaching of Ifa for Iyamooke,
the mother who knows how to nurture,
They said that the child she gave birth to
would not die or be unhealthy.
But the child would not stay with her
after she grew up.
They said she should practice sacrifice so
that the child might have a good life.
She heard and she complied.

Ọlá sílo n'ílé; olá dẹ̀hìn s'ile.
A dífá fún Ìyámọ̀ọ́kẹ́.
Wọ́n ní ọmọ náà tí ó bí kò níí kú
kò níí láìláláàáfíà.
Ṣùgbọ́n ọmọ náà ko níí gbé ọ̀dọ̀ rẹ̀
nígbàtí ó bá dàgbà.
Wọ́n níkí ó wá rúbọ kí ọmọ náà
baà ní ayé rere.
Ó gbọ́; ó rú.

ÒTÚRÁ'BÀRÀ

178

178:1

The hips seem indifferent when they settle down on the mat.
The net works gently, but it holds its goods firmly.
The alukerese vine creeps slowly to maturity.
And when it becomes mature, it turns its face here and there.
This was the teaching of Ifa for Aye, the Earth.
When she was weeping and praying for a child.
They said she would bear a child,
And that the whole world would assemble to serve the child.
They said the child would wear a crown,
But so that she might witness the work of the child in her lifetime,
She should sacrifice for the child.

178:1

Ìdí ṣe bí láìṣúja, nígbàtí ó gúnlẹ̀
lórí ẹní.
Àwọn ṣe jẹ́jẹ́jẹ́jẹ́, ṣùgbọ́n ó mú ẹrù le.
Alukerese rákòròrákòrò ó dàgbà.
Nígbàtí ó dàgbà tán, ó ńṣe ojú rẹ̀
níhìin àti lọ́hùún.
A dá fún Ayé,
Tí ó nf'ẹkún ojú ṣe ìráhùn ọmọ.
Wọ́n ní kí ó bímo,
Kí gbogbo ayé yió máa pé sín
ọmọ náà,
Kí ọmọ yió sì dè ní adé.
Ṣùgbọ́n, kí iṣè rẹ̀ lè ṣe ojú rẹ̀ ni
ìgbà ayé rẹ̀,
Kí ó rúbọ fún ọmọ náà.

ỌKÁNRÀN ÒGÚNDÁ
185

185:1

One who stands ready to act for the good
is supported by Ogun on the day of battle.
A person who cannot fight or talk does not
live long on earth.
Struggle brings respect; struggle brings honor.
This was the teaching of Ifa for Ogungbemi.
They said that even if he does not provoke it,
Whenever the fight comes to him,
He should not run away from it.
It is the powerful who have control
of the world.
No one respects the passive person.
It is the courageous who lay claim
to the world.
People do not give consideration
to the coward.
He was asked to sacrifice.
So that his internal strength would not perish
and his body would remain sound.

185:1

Ẹní ọwọ nyá fún ire ni Ògún igbée
ọjọ́ ijà.
Ẹ̀nìyàn tí kò lè jà, tí kò lè sọ̀rọ̀,
kò níí lè gbé nínú ayé pẹ́.
Ìjà ńsọla; ìjà ńṣe iyì.
A dífá Ògúngbémi.
Wọ́n ní: bí kò tilẹ̀ nii fínràn
nígbàkígbà tí ijà bá dé síi,
Kí ó má maà sá, o.
Alágbára ni ó ní ayé.
Kòsí ẹnití t'ó jẹ́ buyìn fún ọlẹ.
Akin li ó ní ayé.
Wọ́n kíi bù ọlá fún ojo.
Wọ́n níkí ó wá rúbọ.
Kí ìyè inu má ra àti ara líle.

187:1

Not knowing when to fight and when
to withdraw is to be ignorant
of the requirements of courage.
A courageous person who knows how to fight,
But does not know how to withdraw
Will be soundly defeated by another person
of courage in one place or another.
This was the teaching of Ifa for Akinsuyi.
They said he should sacrifice
So that he might know when to avoid and
when not to avoid a battle,
And so that he might be respected always.

ỌKÀNRÀN'SÁ
187

187:1

Má jà, má sá ni àìmọ̀ akin.
Akin tí ó mọ̀ọ́ jà,
Tí ko mọ̀ọ́ sá
A bá akin ibòmíràn lọ.
A dáa fún Akinsuyi.
Wọ́n níkí ó rúbọ,
Kí ó báa lè máà mọ̀ ìgbàtí yẹra àti
àìyẹra fún ìjà,
Kí ó bá lè máà n'íyì lọ́jọ́ gbogbo.

188:1

The teachings of Ifa were interpreted for
Agbonrin, the antelope.
They said that he should sacrifice
So that incidents of insult might not
reach him;
So that he might not die at the hands of
his enemies;
And so that he might be able to save
himself from harm.
He heard but did not sacrifice.
He said his horns were adequate to ward
off suffering.
They said that from far away places,
his enemies would send trouble
that would affect him.
He said his own horns would be enough
to protect him.
But in the end, his horns were not enough.

188:1

A dífá fún Àgbọ̀nrin.
Wọ́n níkí ó rúbọ.
Kí ọ̀ràn ìwọ̀sí tóó dé;
Kí ó má bákú sí owọ́ ọ̀tá;
Kí ó báa lè gbà ara rẹ̀ sílẹ̀.
Ó gbọ́; kò rú.
Ó ní ìwo rẹ̀ tó kọ̀'yà
Wọ́n ní: láti òkèèrè ni ọ̀tá ti má máa ránsé
wá tí yíò máa kàn án lára.
Ó ní: ìwo rẹ̀ ti tó dáàbòbò òun.
Ṣùgbọ́n ìwo rẹ̀ kò tó.

189:1

There is no one whose house cannot become
a place overgrown with grass.
There is no one whose farm cannot become a
rundown place overgrown with
weed and bush.
Right-mindedness will not allow mine to
become an overgrown place.
There is no one whom death cannot kill.
There is no one whose child death cannot kill.
Except for Orunmila, my Lord,
Abiku-Jigbo, one who was born, died,
woke up and lived a long life;
And except for the righteous ones, the
children of Olodumare.

189:1

Kò sẹ̀nití ilé rẹ̀ kò lèe doko.
Kò sẹ̀nití oko rẹ̀ kò lo di ìgbòro.
Òtítọ́ inú kò má jẹ̀kí tèmi doko.
Kò sẹ̀nití ìkú kò lè pa.
Kò sẹ̀nití ìkú kò lè pa ọmọ rẹ̀,
Àfi Ọ̀rúnmìlà, Ólúwa mi,
Àbíkú-jígbó;
À f'àwọn olótítọ́ inú, ọmọ Olódùmarè.

189:2

Fighting in front; fighting behind
If it does not lead to one's death,
It will cause one to become a
courageous person,
One who fights and gains honor,
A person of courage, one who does
battle and wins respect.

Ìjà níwajú, ìjà lẹ́hìn
Bí kò bá pa'ni,
A máà sọ'ni di akin,
Afijàbuyì,
Akin, afijàgbọ̀lá.

191:1

It is through constantly studying Ifa that we
come to understand Ifa.
It is through missing the way that we come
to know the way.
It is the road we have not traveled before
that causes us to wander here and there.

Ifá kí kó níí mú'ni mọ̀ Ifá.
Ọ̀nà ṣísì níí mú'ni mọ̀ ọ̀nà.
Ọ̀nà tí a kò rìn rí,
Níí ṣe'ni ṣìbásìbó.

191:2

Falsehood is not good for anyone.
Commitment breaking is not
good for anyone.
If young people act secretly to
break commitments,
Secret things will happen to them.
This was the teaching of Ifa for an
assistant priest
Who was going to proposition the wife
of the oluwo, the high priest
of Orunmila.

Èké kò sunwọ̀n ara eni.
Ọ̀dàlè kò sunwọ̀n ara eni.
B'ọ́mọdé bá ńyọ́lẹ̀ dà,
Ohun abẹ-'nú á maa yọ́ wọn ṣe.
O dífá fún ajùbòná
Tí ó lọ ńfe obìnrin oluwo.

193:1

The principle of "offend me and I will
offend you,"
Does not allow for the resolution
of a matter.
This was the teaching of Ifa for Olukoya.
They said there is a problem between
him and his relatives,
And that he should sacrifice
So that this problem might not ruin
the harmony among relatives.

"Ṣ'emi ki emi ṣe o,"
Kìí jẹ́kí ọ̀ràn ó tán.
A dífá fún Olúkọ̀yà
Wọ́n ní ọ̀ràn kan wà láàrin òun àti
àwọn ẹbí rẹ̀.
Wọ́n níkí ó wá rúbọ
Kí ọ̀ràn ńaà má lè ba ìrẹ́pọ̀ jẹ́ nínú ẹbí.

ỌKÀNRÀN'ṢẸ̀
197

197:1

A condition of deprivation is not good,
Especially a condition of deprivation which
has never been experienced.
This was the teaching of Ifa for the son
of a person who was once rich.
They said he should sacrifice
So that he would not experience
deprivation also.
The son of the once rich person asked,
"What is deprivation?"
They said: "illness is deprivation."
The son of the formerly rich person asked again,
"What is deprivation?"
They said: "being confined is deprivation, and
being without people is deprivation."
He said that that was enough.
The son of the formerly rich person then
asked what should the sacrifice be?"

ỌKÀNRÀN'ṢẸ̀
197

197:1

Ọ̀ràn ìṣẹ́ kò sunwọ̀n.
Ọ̀ràn ìṣẹ́ kòṣeérí.
A dífá fún ọmọ ọlọ́rọ̀ kan àtijọ́.
Wọ́n níkí ó wá rúbọ.
Kí ọ̀ràn ìṣẹ́ má lè dé síi.
Ọmọ ọlọ́rọ̀ ní: kíni ìṣẹ́?
Wọ́n ní: òkùnrùn ni ìṣẹ́.
Ọmọ ọlọ́rọ̀ ní kíni ìṣẹ́?
Wọ́n ní: akàmọ́ ni ìṣẹ́; àìlénìyàn ni ìṣẹ́
Ó ní: ó tó.
Ọmọ ọlọ́rọ̀ ní kíni ẹbọ?

Ọ̀ṢẸ́ Ọ̀KÀNRÀN
198

198:1

You do not want it. I do not want it.
Deprivation walks alone.
This is the teaching of Ifa for the
unfortunate person.
They said the unfortunate person
should sacrifice
So that s/he might find someone with
whom to walk.

Ìwọ kò fẹ́; èmi kò fẹ́.
Ìṣẹ́ níkan rìn.
A dáa fún olórí burúkú.
Wọ́n níkí olórí burúkú wá rúbọ.
Kí ó báà lè r'éni bá rìn.

200:1

Openly presented and done on behalf
of others.
Openly conducted in the interest of others.
It is Ifa who does things we hear about.
It is only invocations of evil that one
does not know more about.

Pẹ̀rẹ́ ṣìpẹ́; pẹ̀rẹ́ ṣìpe.
Ifá l'ó ṣe ohun tí a bá gbọ́.
Ìgèdè níkan ni kò jù mọ̀.

Ọ̀SÁ'GÚNDÁ
202

202:1

The anthill is the place of deliberation
of the eerun ants.
Asuwa, a grouping together in harmony, is the
place of deliberation of human beings.
It was through the principle of grouping
together that earth was created.
It was through the principle of grouping
together, that heaven was created.
And it was in the form of collectivities that
beings descended on earth.
All inclusive was the grouping together
when beings were first created.
All embracing was the grouping together when
beings were completed.
Formed into collectivities were beings
when they rained down on earth.

Ọ̀SÁ'GÚNDÁ

202

202:1

All goodness became a grouping together
in harmony.
The grouping together of the strands of hair
covered the head.
The grouping together of hairs on the chin
became an object of attention.
The grouping together of trees became a forest.
The grouping together of the eruwa grasses
became a savannah.
The grouping together of the beehives hold up
the roof of the house.
And the grouping together of the ita ants
led to their covering the earth.
Alasuwada, Great Being who creates all beings
in groups, we ask you humbly,
That you grant us things gathered in groups
So that they bring together all things good
for us.

Ọ̀SÁ'GÚNDÁ
202

202:1

Bees form swarms
Eeran plants grow together on the farm.
Brooms are formed from bundles of twigs.
Eeran grass grows in bunches on the plains.
And the elegiri birds form flocks.

It is as a grouping together that we encounter
the grassland.
It is as swarms that the locusts consume
the farm.
It is in several colonies that we find the
termites in their mounds.
It is in groves that we encounter the ekunkun
trees on the water's edge.
It is in clusters we find oore grass at
the riverside.
It is in schools that we find the egbele fish
in the ocean.
It is in groups we encounter the dragon fly.
And the adosusu leaf is never found alone.

Ọ̀SÁ'GÚNDÁ
202

202:1

Dews pouring lightly, pouring lightly
Were used to create the world.
And likewise was done to create the earth.
So that the goodness of togetherness could
come forth at once.
Indeed all goodness took the form of a
gathering together in harmony.

Now, if one ori (mind/heart) encounters good,
It will spread out and touch two hundred.
If my mind/heart is good,
It will spread out and touch you.
And if your mind/heart is good,
It will spread out and touch me.
For if just one mind/heart experiences good,
It will spread out and touch two hundred.

Ọ̀SÁ'GÚNDÁ
202

202:1

Àgìrìyàn ni mọrẹ̀rẹ̀ eèrùn.
Aṣùwà ni mọrẹ̀rẹ̀ ènìyàn.
Aṣùwà dá ayé.
Aṣùwà dá Ọrun.
Aṣùwà dàa sílẹ̀
Àsẹkún ṣùwàdà nígbàtí ìwà ṣe.
Àsẹkún ṣùwàdà nígbàtí ìwà gún.
Aṣùwà nígbà ìwà rọ̀ọ̀.

Ire gbogbo wá d'àṣùwà.
Irún pé ṣùṣù, wọ́n gborí.
Irún àgbọ̀n pé ṣùṣù, wọ́n di òjòntarigi.
Igí pé ṣùṣù, wọ́n di igbó.
Erúwà pé ṣùṣù, wọ́n dọ̀dàn.
Agbọ́n pé ṣùṣù fówó tilé.
Ìtà pé ṣùṣù bó ilẹ̀.
Aláṣùwàdà, a pé ọ́
Kó O rán ìwà ṣùṣù wáá
Kí wọn kó ire gbogbo wáá bá wa.

202:1

Aṣùwà ni toyin
Aṣùwà leéran ńhù nínú oko.
Aṣùwà ni tò ṣùṣù ọ́wọ̀
Aṣùwà leéran ńhù nínú aáre
Aṣùwà ni ti Ẹlẹ́gírí

Aṣùwà làá bọ́dàn
Aṣùwà leṣú ńfiijoko.
Aṣùwà ọ̀pọ̀ sùùù làá bá ikán nínú ògán.
Aṣùwà làá bá ekunkun létí omi
Aṣùwà làá bá òòré lódò
Aṣùwà làá bá lámilámi.
Aṣùwà làá bẹjá ẹ́gbẹlẹ lókun
Ewé adóṣùṣú kìí dúró lóun nìkan

Ìrì tu wílí, tu wílí
Lafi dálé ayé
La bù dá ile

202:1

Kíre ṣùṣù kó wá ṣù pírípírí.
Ire gbogbo d'aṣùwà.

Ǹjé, bórí kan bá sunwọ̀n,
A ràn igba.
Orí mi tó sunwọ̀n,
Ló ràn yìn.
Orí yín tó sunwọ̀n
Ló ràn mí.
Bórí kan bá sunwọ̀n
A ràn igba.

ÌKÁ ÒGÚNDÁ
204

204: 1

Ogun causes me to be vindicated.
Ogun, please support me.
There is no one who has a problem or
a struggle
Who should not ask that Ogun please
support her.
One who does good will receive good.
Surely a good person is one whom Ogun
will support.
This was the teaching of Ifa for Adetutu,
Offspring of the coward who
breathes fearfully,
He who was half dead before the
struggle began.
They said he should sacrifice
He heard but did not comply.

204

204: 1

Ògún dá mi láre.
Ògún jọ̀wọ́; gbe mí.
Kòsí enití ó ni ejọ́; tàbí ìjà
Tí kìí wípé kí Ògún jọ̀wọ́ gbé òun.
Ẹnití ńṣe rere á rí ire.
Dandan, ẹnirere ni ti Ògún yió gbé.
A dífá fún Adétútú
Ọmọ ojo k'ó f'ọkàn bá lẹ̀mi,
A kú dé' dajì kí ìjà tó dé.
Wọn níkí ó rúbọ.
Ó gbọ́; ó rúbọ.

206:1

It is when they are young that we
should prune the branches
of the iroko tree.
For when they are fully grown,
We will have to make greater sacrifice.
This was the teaching of Ifa for Otu,
the mother who was still breast
feeding her child.

Kérékéré li a tii pẹ̀ka iroko.
Bí ó bá dàgbà tán,
A máà gbà ẹbọ.
A dáa fún Ótú, abiyamo.

ÒGÚNDÁ'TÚRÁ
207

207:1

It is a good head that overcomes
the opponent.
It is the impaired head that the opponent
renders completely powerless.
Who is one with an impaired head?
It is one whom the world constantly blocks
And he says there is no one who can block
him until he dies.
He, indeed, is the one with the impaired head.

Orí rere ni ṣẹ́gun ọ̀tá̩.
Orí àìsàn li ọ̀tá i di li adipa
Tani íjẹ́ orí àlàìsàn?
Ẹnití ayé ńdì
Tí ó ní kòsí ẹnití ó lè di òun li àdìpa
Òun, nii jẹ́ orí-àìsàn.

208:1

They have done great wrong to me,
but I am not ruined.
The strength of their arms do not match mine.
They curse; they swear and they wish me evil.
But Otura Ogunda says that I should not fear.
He says that I should not be timid.
He says that he will mend my ways,
And that my life will be good.
It is Otura Ogunda who will touch my
head gently for me,
So that no curse may harm me;
So that no swearing may harm me;
So that no charm may harm me;
So that no evil wish may harm me.

208: 1

Wọ́n semísemí ṣùgbọ́n èmi kò bàjé.
Apá wọn kò ká tèmi.
Wọ́n nṣ'èpè; wọ́n ńgegún;
wọ́n nfẹ́ ibi sí mi.
Òtúrá Ògúndá ní kí èmi má bẹ̀rù.
Ó ní kí mo mà s'ojo.
Kí a bámi tún tèmi ṣe.
Kí ayé tèmi á dára.
Òtúrá Ògúndá li ó wẹ́ orí tèmi fún mi,
Kí èègún má mú mi,
Kí èpè má mú mi,
Kí èèdi má mú mi,
Kí ẹ̀fún má mú mi.

ÒGÚNDÁ ÌRẸTẸ̀

209

209:1

Sweet potato with fresh leaves might seem
like a powerful potion.
And an abundance of magical medicine tends
to intoxicate the possessor.
But even if you have a multitude of powerful
potions,
If you are dishonest,
Your dishonesty will undermine their
effectiveness.
Surely, kindness will be more effective than
such potions.
This was the teaching of Ifa for
King Alanak'esuu,
One who dared not reject the advice of Ifa.

209:1

Kúkúndùkún a b'ewé gẹrugẹru dàbí
oògùn l'ágbára.
Ọ̀pọ̀ oògùn a gun'mo gàlègàlè.
Ṣùgbọ́n bí ó bá l'ọ́pọ̀ oògún,
Bí ó bá l'ékèé,
Èké ò níí jẹ́ ó jẹ.
Dandan, inúrere jẹ́ ju ewé lọ.
Dífá fún Ọ̀ọ̀ni Alànàk'èsùú,
Èyítí kò gbọ́dọ̀ kọ̀ ọ̀rọ̀ Ifá sílẹ̀.

Ọ̀ṢẸ́ Ò̀GÚNDÁ
212

212:1

Ifa does not recognize king or queen.
Poverty does not recognize beauty.
The machete does not recognize its maker.
And on the day the guest is extremely hungry,
His eyes search unashamedly through
the house and through the farm.
This is the teaching of Ifa interpreted for a king,
Who sold his jeweled crown for a simple dish
of green vegetables.

Ifá kò mọ̀ ọba okùnrin tàbí ọba obìnrin.
Òsì kò mọ̀ ẹ̀wà.
Àgada kò m'ojú ẹnití ó rọ'hun.
Ebi ọjọ́ kan pa ọmọ àlejò,
Ojú rẹ̀ tó'lé; ojú rẹ̀ tó'ko.
Dífá fún Ọlọ́fin
Tí a tà adé èsurú j'ẹ̀fọ́.

ÒFÚN'GÚNDÁ

214

214:1

A marshy place puts forth a soft chest.
This was the teaching of Ifa for Orunmila
Who was suffering losses on all sides for a very long time.
They said that he should practice sacrifice,
So that during the year, the Lord of Heaven might compensate him for all his losses.
He sacrificed and found wealth.
When those who had joined him to eat the day before came to greet him saying
"Greetings for being generous" and "the Lord of Heaven will transform your losses into riches,"
Orunmila answered, saying that the losses he had suffered in the past
Did not equal the wealth he had gained.
Ifa says that someone has been suffering losses in the past;
But this year the Lord of Heaven will transform her losses into gain
And everything that has been lost from her hand
Will return to her purse.

ÒFÚN'GÚNDÁ

214

214:1

Àbatà obaya gbẹdẹgbẹdẹ.
A dá fún Ọ̀rúnmìlà
Tí ó ti ńṣe òfo ẹ̀gbẹ́lẹ̀gbẹ́ láílái.
Wọ́n ní kí ó rúbọ.
Pé ní ọdún yìí ni Ọlọ́run san gbogbo
ohun rẹ̀ tí ó ti ńṣe òfo fún un.
Ó rúbo ó sì rí olà.
Nígbàtí àwọn tí ó bá jẹun ni àná wá kí pé
"Ẹ kú ìnáwó" àti pé "Ọlọ́run yió sọ
òfo rẹ di ọrọ̀,"
Ọ̀rúnmìlà dáhùn ó ní òfo tí ṣe láná kò tó
olà tí ó ti jèrèe.
Ifá ní ẹníkan tí ńṣe òfo rí,
Ṣùgbọ́n ni ọdún yìí ni Ọlọ́run yió sọ òfo
náà di èrè.
Tí gbogbo ohun tí ó ti sonù lọ́wọ́ rẹ̀
Yió bọ̀ sí àpo rẹ̀ pátápátá.

216:1

Bad character causes one to become
a coward.
This was the teaching of Ifa for the thief.
They said that a thief is not as courageous
as an owner.
They said the thief should sacrifice
So that he might accept the gentle way
to acquire things.
But he would not sacrifice.

Ìwà burúkú ńmu'ni s'ojo.
A dífá fún olè.
Wọ́n níkí olè kò máa láìyà bí olóhun.
Wọ́n níkí olè wá rúbọ.
Kí ó bá lè máa gbà ọ̀nà ẹ̀sọ̀ ni ńnkan.
Kò rúbọ.

Ọ̀SÁ'Ọ̀TÚRÁ
219

219:1

Osa Otura asks what is truth?
I ask what is truth?
Orunmila says truth is the Lord of Heaven
who guides the world rightly.
Osa Otura asks what is truth?
I ask what is truth?
Orunmila says truth is the Unseen One
guiding the world in the right way,
The wisdom that Olodumare uses,
great wisdom, abundant wisdom.
Osa Otura asks what is truth?
I ask what is truth?
Orunmila says truth is the nature
of Olodumare.
Truth is the word that cannot fall.

219:1

Ifa is truth.
Truth is the word that cannot be ruined.
A great power superior to all, an
everlasting good.
Speak truth; do justice.
Speak truth and do justice constantly.
Those who do right the divine ones will sustain.

219:1

Ọsá Òtúrá ní kíni òtító?
Èmi ní kíni òtító?
Ọrúnmìlà ní:òtító ni Olúwa Ọrun ti ńtọ ayé.
Ọsá Òtúrá ní kíni òtító?
Èmi ní kíni òtító?
Ọrúnmìlà ní: òtító ni Ẹni-àìrí ńtọ ayé.
Ọgbọ́n ti Olódùmare ńlo, ọgbọ́n ńlá,
ọ̀pọ̀lọ́pọ̀ ọgbọ́n.
Ọsá Òtúrá ní kíni òtító?
Ọrúnmìlà ní òtító ni ìwà Olódùmarè.
Òtító ni ọ̀rọ̀ ti kò lè ṣubú.
Ifá ni òtító.
Òtító ni ọ̀rọ̀ ti kò lè bàjé.
Agbára ńlá, ajùlo, ire àìlópin.
S'òtító; ṣ'òdodo.
S'òtító; o sì tún ṣ'òdodo.
Ẹnití ṣ'òtító ni imàle yió gbè, o.

221:1

If one who sleeps alone sleeps badly,
Only the Lord of Heaven can wake him
while he sleeps.
This was the teaching of Ifa for the stranger
Who was going to a field to stand,
So that he might ask someone to help him
to lift a load on his head.
They said he should sacrifice.
He heard and complied.
The stranger went into the field and secured
his load on the ground.
He looked forward but he saw no one.
He looked backwards and he saw no one.
He said, "This load has, indeed, become the
load of the Lord of Heaven.

221:1

Now, strong wind help me lift this load
onto my head.
Don't you know that one who has no one,
The Lord of Heaven is the one on whom
that person relies."

221 : 1

Anìkànsùn bí ó bá sùn sí aburadi,
Ọlọ́run níkan níí jíi lójú oorun.
A dáa fún àjèjì tí ó lọ sí ẹlùjù ni ó ìdúró,
Kí ó bá bèèrè ẹ́ni bá òun gbé ẹrù dé orí
Wọ́n níkí ó rú.
Ó gbọ́; ó rúbọ
Àjèjì dé inú ẹlùjù ó di ẹrù kálẹ̀
Ó wò iwájú kò rí eníkan.
Ó wò ẹ̀hìn kò rí eníkan.
Ó ní: ẹrù yìí mà di ẹrù Ọlọ́run o.
Ǹjé efúùfù líle bá mi gbé ẹrù yìí d'órí
Èyin kò mọ̀ pé ẹnití kò ní ará,
Ọlọ́run ni agbójúlé olúwarè?

222:1

When the head is full of hair,
We call the barber.
When the river has risen in flood,
We call the ferryman.
And if the ferryman does not carry us across,
Then we row straight across the river ourselves.
We row across the water anyway.

Órí l'ó kún,
Ni a npe alábe.
Odò l'ó kún,
L'a npè òtukọ̀.
Òtukọ̀ kò bá tù,
Àwa a tu odò looró gangan.
Àwa tu ojú omi ṣánkálá.

222:2

One who guards against treachery is not
overly fearful.
After all, when honey bees are finished,
they leave a honeycomb in the house.
But when soldier ants are finished,
they leave devastation.
This was the teaching of Ifa for the people of
earth and the inhabitants of heaven
When they were warring with each other.

Ẹnití r'ọ̀tẹ̀ sá kò ṣ'ojo
Oyin ṣe tán, fáfárá dé'lé.
Eerùn ṣe tán, f'àgàn dé'lé.
A dífá aráyé a bu fún ará ọ̀run
Nígbàtí wọ́n ńgbógun sí ara won.

222:3

The teachings of Ifa were interpreted for
Akere Kokeyo, the frog, the child
of the King of Oyo.
They said two blessings were coming to him,
And that he should sacrifice so that both
blessings might reach him.
But Akere refused to sacrifice.
He said when he saw the blessings,
he would sacrifice.
He was at the farm when they came to tell
him his wife had given birth to a child.
When Akere heard this, he was exceedingly
happy.
He said that before he went home, he would
tap some palm wine.
Then, a messenger from the house arrived to
say that some people came to call
on Akere at home,

222:3

Because the king had passed and they wanted
to give him the title.
They found Akere on the farm where he
was tapping palm wine at the
top of a palm tree.
When they told Akere, he was so happy
to accept
He forgot that he was up in the palm tree.
And he fell down and broke his arms and legs.
They took him home.
But when they tried to cure him and could not,
They gave the title to another person and left
Akere alone.
Since that day, people have been saying:
"Happiness, too much happiness,
broke the frog's legs."

222:3

A dá fún Àkeré kokẹyọ ti iṣe ọmọ Oniṣinkọ.
Wọ́n ni ire méjì nbọ̀wá baa
Kí ó rúbọ kí méjèèjì le tẹ̀ẹ́ lọ́wọ́
Àkeré kọ̀ kò rúbọ.
Ó ní ìgbàtí òun bá rí ire náà, òun yió wá rúbọ.
Oko ni Àkeré wà, ìbẹ̀ ní wọ́n sí gbé wá sọ fún
un pé aya rẹ̀ bí ọmọ.
Nígbàtí Àkeré gbọ́ èyí, inú rẹ̀ dùn púpọ̀
Ó ní kí òun tó lọ sílé, òun yió dá ẹmu òun náà.
Léhìnnáà oníṣẹ́ ti ilé dé wípé wọ́n ńpe
Àkeré nílé
Nítoríti ọba kú,wọ́n fẹ́ fi Àkeré joyè.
Wọ́n lọ bá Àkeré nínú oko níbití ó gbé ńdá
ẹmu ní orí ọ̀pẹ.
Nígbàtí wọ́n so fún Àkeré, inú rẹ̀ dùn tó bẹ̀
gẹ̀ tí ó fi jẹ́-pé.

222:3

Ó gbàgbé pé orí ọ̀pe ni ó wà.
Ó sì wólulẹ̀ ó sì fi apá àti itan ṣẹ́
Wọ́n gbéé wá sílẹ̀.
Nígbàtí wọ́n wòó tí kò ṣe wò sàn,
Wọ́n fi elòmíran joyé náà wọ́n sì fi Àkeré sílẹ̀.
Láti ọjọ́ náà ni wọ́n ti máà nwípé;
Ayọ̀, ayọ̀ jù,Àkeré f'itan ṣẹ́.

223:1

The tradition which the father of
a child follows,
Is the one which the child practices.
This was the teaching of Ifa for Oluigbo.
The same was given to Oluodan.
They said they should sacrifice.
Oluigbo was the one who sacrificed.
They said that all good would gather
in his hands.
And people would come to receive it.

Àsà tí baba ọmọ ńṣe,
Ni ọmọ íhù ni.
A dífá fún Olúigbó
A bù fún Olúọ̀dàn
Wọ́n níkí àwọn wá rúbọ.
Olúigbó ni ó rú.
Wọ́n ní gbogbo ire ni o máà pé sí ọwọ́ rẹ̀
Tí wọ́n máa maa wá gbàá.

223:2

Osa does not offend.
Osa does not injure.
The one who we thought offended us,
did not do us harm.
This was the teaching of Ifa for Owa,
Who was seeing a person as a thief,
When in fact that person had not done
any harm.
They said that Owa should sacrifice,
So that Eshu might not punish him
For falsely accusing a person who did
nothing wrong.

223:2

Ọ̀sá kò ṣẹ́.
Ọ̀sá kò ro.
Ẹnití a rò pé ó s'ẹni, kò s'ẹni.
A dífá fún Ọwa.
Ọwa ńfi ojú olè
Wo eníkan ti kò ṣẹ́
Wọ́n níkí ó wá rúbọ
Kí Ẹ̀sù má bá tìí lọ.
Dúnrumọ́ ènìyàn kan ṣaa tí kò ṣẹ̀ẹ́.

Ọ̀SÀ OFÚN
225

225:1

We avoid the snake so that the snake
might not bite us.
We avoid the elephant so that the elephant
might not seize us.
We avoid the buffalo so that the buffalo
might not fight with us.
We avoid fire so that fire might not burn us.
We avoid debt so that people
might not ridicule us.
We avoid other people's property so that we
might not become thieves.
And so that one day people, without warning,
will not yell out at us.
We avoid charms so that the evil words of
charms might not affect us.
They said that those who do not
avoid anything whatsoever on earth,

Ọ̀SÀ OFÚN
225

225:1

There will be no pleasantness for them.
And they will not live long on earth.
This was the teaching of Ifa for humans.
They said that humans should sacrifice
So that they might know what to avoid
which is called *eewo, that which is forbidden*.
They said "those of you who sacrifice will
live long on earth."

225:1

À ńsá fún ejò kí ejò má báa bù'ni je.
À ńsá fún erin kí erin má báa mú'ni.
À ńsá fún ẹfòn kí ẹfòn má lè bá'ni jà.
À ńsá fún iná kí iná má lè jó'ni.
À ńsá fún igbèsè kí ọmọ aráyé máa báá
fi'ni ṣe ẹlẹ́yà.
À ńsá fún ohun olóhun kí a má báá di olè
Níjọ́kan àìròtẹ́lẹ̀ kí a má báa pariwo lẹ́ni.
À ńsá fún àlé kí ọ̀rọ̀ burúkú àlé má báá mú'ni.
Àwọn tí ó wà ti wípé àwọn kìí sáfún
ohunkóhun nínú ayé,
Adún kòsí fún wọn.
À jẹ pẹ́ ayé kòsí.
A dáa fún àwọn ènìyàn.
Wọ́n níkí àwọn ènìyàn wá rúbọ
Kí wọ́n lè màá mọ̀ ohun tí a isáfún
Tí à ńpè ni èèwọ̀.
Wọ́n ní: ẹ̀yin tí ẹ rúbọ á pé nínú ayé
Àti ayé á màá dún fún yin.

235:1

They said that Olobahun Ijapa should sacrifice.
So that he might be given a great gift.
He refused and did not sacrifice.
They said, "One who does not give something
from himself
Will not receive something for himself
from others."

Wọ́n níkí Ọlọ́bahun Íjàpá rú
Kí wọ́n baà lè máa mú ẹ̀bùn ńlá wá fún un.
Ó kò kò rú.
Wọ́n ní: Ẹnití kò mú ohun t'ọwọ́ rẹ̀ wá,
Kìí ri tẹni gbà sọ́wọ́.

ÒTÚRÚPỌ̀N ṢẸ́
241

241:1

The world is not pleasant enough to
live in forever.
It is the child who says that the world
is nice enough.
This was the teaching of Ifa for Orunmila,
And likewise for the people.
They said that Orunmila should sacrifice,
So that the world might be pleasant for people.
Orunmila asked: "If they themselves do not do
things for themselves,
How can they truly experience the enjoyment
of being in the world?"
They said: "A child acts so that a child may eat;
But the father of the child teaches the child
how to act so the child might eat."
Orunmila understood and sacrificed.
Then they said humans should sacrifice so
that it might benefit them.
They came to sacrifice little by little.
Those who sacrifice will have enjoyable life.

ÒTÚRÚPỌ̀N ṢẸ́

241

241:1

Ayé kò dùn tó ibití à ígbé títí.
Ọmọdé ni ó ńwípé ayé dára tó.
A dáa fún Ọ̀rúnmìlà
A bù fún àwọn ènìyàn.
Wọ́n níkí Ọ̀rúnmìlà wá rúbọ.
Kí ayé lè màá dùn fún àwọn ènìyàn.
Ọ̀rúnmìlà ní: bí wọ́n kò bá tìkálará wọn
ṣe ohun ara wọn,
Wọ́n ha lè mọ̀ adún ní ayé báwo?
Wọ́n ní: ọmọ a ṣe kí ọmọ íje;
Baba ọmọ nii kọ́ ọmo jẹ.
Ọ̀rúnmìlà gbọ́; ó rú.
A níkí àwọn ènìyàn wá ṣe ẹbọ tí ó kàn wọ́n.
Wọ́n ńwa díẹ̀díẹ̀
Ẹnití ó bá ṣ'ẹbọ ayé rẹ̀ á dùn.

ÒTÚRÚPỌ̀N OFÚN
243

243:1

Ifa teachings were interpreted for the osan tree.
They said that the osan tree should give
food to others,
And that she should give drink to others.
They said that the osan tree would never come
to an end, if she sacrificed.
They said she should, therefore, sacrifice.
She heard and complied.
They said anyone who has much,
Should share some of it with those who
are still searching.
May it be that we see the ancestors again.
And may we also never come to an end.

243:1

A dífá fún igi-ọsàn.
Wọ́n níkí igi-ọsàn máa fún wọn je.
Kí ó máa fún wọn mu.
Wọ́n níkí igi-ọsàn kó máa yéé ni, bí ó bá rúbọ.
Wọ́n níkí ó rúbọ.
Ó gbọ́; ó rúbọ.
Wọ́n níkí ẹnití ó bá ní púpò,
Kí ó fi díẹ̀ fún ẹnití kòi tí ní tí ó ńwákiri.
Tó a bá rí won.
Àwa sì yóò máa yè ni.

245:1

Reconstruct yourself.
If we are given birth, we should bring
ourselves into being again.
The balanced person. The moderate person.
One who knows moderation will not fall
into disgrace.
I ask "who knows moderation?"
Orunmila says "One who is always working."
I ask "who knows moderation?"
Orunmila says "one who does not
squander money."
I ask "who knows moderation?"
Orunmila says "one who dares not steal."
I ask "who knows moderation?"
Orunmila says "one who does not owe
excessive debts."

Òtúrá Rẹtẹ́
245

245:1

I ask "who knows moderation?"
Orunmila says "one who does not drink liquor;"
One who does not break commitments
to a friend;
One who wakes early in the morning, meditates
and thinks deeply about one's actions."
From among the thorns and thistles, the palm
leaf emerges pointing upward.
A balanced person is an *ameso*,
one who is truly thoughtful in conduct.

245:1

Tún'ra rẹ tè.
Bí a bí'ni, àá tún'ra ẹni bí.
Àmúwọ̀n. Àmúwọ̀n.
Ení mọ ìwọ̀n, kìí tẹ̀
Èmi ní taní mọ̀'wọ̀n?
Ọ̀rúnmìlà ní ẹnití ńṣiṣẹ́
Èmi ní taní mọ̀'wọ̀n?
Ọ̀rúnmìlà ní ẹnitì kìí náwó ọwọ́ rè tán.
Èmi ní taní mọ̀'wọ̀n?
Ọ̀rúnmìlà ní ẹnití kò jẹ́ jalè.
Èmi ní taní mọ̀'wọ̀n?
Ọ̀rúnmìlà ní ẹnití kìí je gbèsè rékọjà
Èmi ní taní mọ̀'wọ̀n?
Ọ̀rúnmìlà ní ẹnití kìí mu ọtí;
Ẹnití kò jẹ́ dalẹ̀ ọ̀rẹ́;
Ojíkùtùkùtù bánú ara rẹ̀ ṣírò nítorí ìṣe rẹ̀
Nínú ẹ̀gún nínú ìṣó, màrìwò ọ̀pẹ yọ rí sókè.
Àmúwọn ni amẹ̀ṣọ́.

ỌṢẸ́ ÒTÚRÁ
248

248:1

The teachings of Ifa were interpreted
for the 200 divine powers on the
right side of the Lord of Heaven.
And the same was done for the 200
divine powers on the left side of
the Lord of Heaven.
Who came to earth with Oshun, the elegant
one, possessor of the beautiful
coral comb,
In order to prepare the world for all creatures.
But when they arrived on earth, they did
not want to give Oshun due respect.
So, Oshun began to use her secret power to
render ineffective the efforts of the
400 divine powers.
They quickly went to Olodumare.
They prepared their case and presented it
to him.

Ọ̀ṢẸ́ Ọ̀TÚRÁ
248

248:1

They told him that everything that he had
told them to go and do,
They could not accomplish it.
Olodumare asked them: "what about Oshun,
the only female among you?"
Then he asked "did you give her due respect?"
They said they did not give her due respect.
Olodumare said that they should go and
give Oshun due respect.
They returned to earth and they began to
give due respect to Oshun.
Then, all their deliberations and efforts
began to go right.
Thus, we give due respect to Oshun,
Our mother who is always present.

248: I

Dífá fún igba Irúnmọlẹ̀ ojùkọ̀tún Ọlọ́run,
A bù fún igba Irúnmọlẹ̀ ojùkọ̀si Ọlọ́run,
Tí wọ́n bọ̀wa ilé ayé pẹ̀lú Ọ̀ṣun Ṣẹ̀ẹ̀gẹ̀sí
Olóòya-iyùn,
Láti pèsè ilé ayé fún gbogbo ẹ̀dá.
Nígbàtí wọ́n dé ilé ayé,wọ́n kò fẹ́ẹ́
fímò ṣe t'Ọ̀ṣun.
Ǹjẹ́ Ọ̀ṣun bẹ̀rẹ̀ sí gbé ìkọ̀kọ̀ ba ẹbọ Irúnmọle jẹ́.
Gbogbo èro àti íṣe wọn sí kùnà.
Wọ́n gbéra; wọ́n lọ òdò Olódùmarè.
Wọ́n k'ẹ́jọ́; wọ́n rò fún Olódùmarè.
Wọ́n ní gbogbo ohun tí ó ní wọn lọ ṣe,
Wọ́n ní kò ṣeé ṣe.
Olódùmarè ní: "Ọ̀ṣun, obinrin kan tí ńbe
láarín yin ńkọ́?"
Ó ní ǹjé, "ẹ fìmọ̀ ṣe tirẹ̀?"

Ọ̀ṢẸ́ ÒTÚRÁ
248

248: I

Wọ́n ní àwọn ó fìmọ̀ ṣe tirẹ̀
Olódùmarè níkí wọ́n lọ fìmọ̀ ṣe tirè.
Wọ́n wá padà wá sílé ayé.
Wọ́n wá fìmọ̀ ṣe t'Ọ̀ṣun
Nígbànáà gbogbo èro àti ìṣe
wọn bẹ̀rẹ̀ síí gún.
Nítorínáà, a fìmọ̀ jẹ́ t'Ọ̀ṣun
Yèyé wa a bá wọ́n pé nímò.

248:1

ÀSỌYÉ

This is a teaching on the indispensability of the female presence and principle in existence and in all things of importance to the world as a whole. It immediately reminds us of Anna Julia Cooper's teaching that "there is a female as well as male side to truth" and that those who do not recognize and respond appropriately to this do, damage to both male and female, as well as to the world. The critical nature of the teaching is accentuated by several elements. First, the composition of the workforce sent to set the world right is a ratio of 400 to one. We can read this in at least two ways: first, as an indication that the issue is woman/female whether one or 1,000. Also the lesson is that the *aṣẹ* of one who is right is greater than the larger number and power of those who are wrong. Secondly, the teaching is about the very work of creation of the world, and thus essential to how we understand both its foundation and functioning.

Thirdly, the point of the indispensability of the female element in existence and the world is reaffirmed not only by Oshun's ability to thwart and make successful the work of creation, but by the divine direction to the male divinities to return to earth and give Oshun due respect. That Olodumare, Lord of Heaven and Earth, gave this specific direction carries with it an unsurpassable authority for the moral necessity of the due respect and respectful inclusion of the female in all matters of importance in the world. Olodumare's two questions before giving the direction to respect and include Oshun in the work of creation are instructive and rich in symbolism. First, he asks what about Oshun, the one female among them. The question at once suggests that in their report the male divinities did not even mention Oshun. Therefore, Olodumare first compels them by his question to recognize her very presence in the creation process.

Secondly, he asks them did they give her due respect? The first and second questions are linked and both are about respectful recognition and inclusion. But the first question is to indicate that basic recognition of the female presence and principle in the serious activity of world creation is the beginning basis of respect for female as female, woman as woman. The second question makes it morally compelling to recognize and respect the personal and general worth of women as partners in any process and project of bringing good into the world. Here *due respect* is clearly a question of respect for both the presence and power of women. For their presence and participation determine not only the *quality of the process* but also the *success of the project*. This point is made clear in this text but also in Odu Osa Meji (10:2) which states that men can do nothing *of substance* in the world without the participation of women.

The lesson here, again, is that in all things essential, women and men are and must be partners in the constant co-creation of the world. And thus, we are morally compelled to ask in every important and essential activity, the two questions Olodumare asks: first, what about the woman, where is she in the process or project, and secondly, do we give her due respect as a person and indispensable partner in the ongoing project and process of bringing good into the world?

250

250:1

The liar casts the kola nut and it
yields a bad omen.
The commitment breaker casts the kola nut
and it does not yield a good result.
But the good-hearted person casts the
kola nut and the result is clearly
promising.

Èké pa'bi, ó dí.
Ọ̀dàlẹ̀ pa'bi, kò yàn.
Onínúre pa'bi, ó yé peregede.

253:1

The teachings of Ifa were interpreted
for one who is familiar with wealth
and is not ungenerous.
They said he should come forth and sacrifice.
They said he should sacrifice everything
that the mouth consumes.
He heard and made the sacrifice.
And he prospered accordingly.
They said that a kindhearted person will not
suffer from need in the world.

A dífá fún anímọ̀-ọlà anímáṣahun
Wọ́n níkí ó wá rúbọ.
Wọ́n níkí ohun gbogbo tí ẹnú ijẹ ni kí ó wá rú.
Ó gbọ́; ó rúbọ.
Ó sì ṣe aásìkí bẹ̀ẹ̀ gẹ́gẹ́.
Wọ́n níkí olóore kíí ṣe àìnì layé.

254:1

They taught me and then I taught
myself again.
This was the interpretation of Ifa for Oluseso,
the one who practices gentleness.
They said "that which is good in the eyes of the
whole world is what Oluseso would
like to do."
They said he should sacrifice,
So that the people of the world might have
respect for him.
He heard and made the sacrifice.

Wọ́n tẹ̀ mí; mo túnra mi tẹ̀.
A dífá fún Olùṣẹ̀sọ̀.
Wọ́n ní: èyítí ó dára lójú ayé ni yió
máa wù Olùṣẹ̀sọ̀ láti ṣe.
Wọ́n ní ó wá rúbọ
Ki àwọn ọmọ aráyé lè máa buyìn fún un.
Ó gbọ́; ó rú.

254:2

The teaching of Ifa was interpreted
for Omi, water.
They said that he should sacrifice.
They said that no one would ever become
his enemy.
He understood and sacrificed.
They said anyone who makes himself
an enemy of water
Will die a premature death.

A dífá fún Omi.
Wọ́n níkí ó wá rúbọ.
Wọ́n ní: ẹnikẹ́ni kó máà ṣ'ọ̀tá rẹ̀ láíláí.
Ó gbọ́; ó rú.
Wọ́n ní: ẹnití ó ńbá Omi ṣọ̀tá,
Ni yíò kú ikú àìtọ́jọ́.

Ọ̀ṢẸ́ OFÚN
255

255:1

If one's destiny is unfortunate, perhaps one's
internal wisdom is not sufficient.
There is water in the house of the owner
of the ocean.
The ocean is the head of all waters.
There is water in the house of the owner of
the lagoon, the lagoon which holds
second place.
There is wisdom within Akoda,
Akoda who taught the whole world Ifa.
There are words within Asheda, Asheda who
taught all the elders wise counsel.
There is wisdom within Orunmila,
He who makes the world right,
The repairer who repairs the unfortunate
destiny.

Ọ̀ṢẸ́ OFÚN
255

255:1

The one who improves perception that
is not good.
This was the teaching of Ifa for those who
did not know what to do and did not
know what to be,
Who were crying out every day about lacking
a good destiny.
They said that those who do not know
what to do and do not know what to be,
If they study Ifa, their destinies, in the end,
will be good.

255:1

Bí orí kò sunwọ̀n, bóyá ọgbọ́n inú ni kò ìtó.
Omi ńbe nílé Olokun.
Okun ńbe olórí omi.
Omi ńbe nílé olọ́sà, ọ̀sà ibìkéjì.
Ọgbọ́n ńbe nínú Akọ́dá,Akọ́dá tí nkọ́
gbogbo ayé n'Ífá.
Ọ̀rọ̀ ńbe nínú Aṣèdá,Aṣèdá tí nkọ́
gbogbo àgbà ni ìmọ́ràn.
Ọgbọ́n ńbe nínú Ọ̀rúnmìlà, amáyégún,
Ò dúdú tí ńdú orí emèrè,
A tún rí tí kò sunwọ̀n ṣe.
A dáa fún àwọn kòmọ̀ọ̀ṣe-kòmọ̀ọ̀wà
Tí ojoojúmọ́ kégbe orí áìsùnwọ̀n.
Wọ́n ní: àwọn kòmọ̀ọ́ṣe-kòmọ̀ọ́wà
Tí wọ́n kọ́ Ifá, orí wọn á sunwọ̀n nígbẹ̀hìn.

Òfún Ṣẹ́

256

256:1

Ifa says there is someone whom people say
will never be important.
But the Lord of Heaven will open the way to
wealth and peace for her/him.
Everyone will return repeatedly to pay honor
to her/him.
And they will bow down to her/him.
And even if s/he does not acquire a title,
S/he will be honored more than those who
do have titles.

256:1

Ifá ní ẹnìkan wà tí àwọn ènìyàn ńsọ pé
kò ní láárí.
Ṣùgbọ́n Ọlọ́run máa sí ọ̀nà ọlà àti
àlàáfíà fún un.
Gbogbo ènìyàn ni yió máa padà láti wa tún bu
ọlà fún un.
Tí wọ́n yió sì máa tẹ orí balẹ̀ fún un.
Bí kò jọyè,
Òun yíò ní ọlà ju ẹnití ó jọyè lọ.

Resources

Abimbola, Wande. 1975. *Sixteen Great Poems of Ifá, UNESCO.*

Abimbola, Wande. 1975. *Ìwàpẹ̀lẹ̀:* The Concept of Good Character in Ifá Literary Corpus, in *Yoruba Oral Tradition: Poetry in Music, Dance and Drama*, (ed.) W. Abimbola, Ilé-Ifẹ̀, Nigeria: Department of African Languages and Literatures, University of Ifẹ̀.

Abimbola, Wande. 1976. *Ifá: An Exposition of the Ifá Literary Corpus*, Ìbàdàn, Nigeria: Oxford University Press.

Abimbola, Wande. 1977. *Àwọn Ọmọ Ojú Odù Mẹ̀rẹ̀ẹ̀rìndílógún*, Ìbàdàn, Nigeria: Oxford University Press.

Abimbola, Wande. 1977. *Ifá Diviniation Poetry*, New York: London, Lagos: Nok Publishers.

Abimbola, Wande. 1997. *Ifá Will Mend Our Broken Ways: Thoughts on Yoruba Religion and Culture in Africa and the Diaspora*, Roxbury, MA: Aim Books.

Abiodun, Rowland. 1975. "Ifá Art Objects: An Interpretation Based on Oral Tradition," in *Yoruba Oral Tradition: Poetry in Music, Dance, and Drama,* (ed.) Wande Abimbola, Ilé-Ifẹ̀, Nigeria: Department of African Languages and Literature, University of Ifẹ̀.

Abiodun, Rowland. 1983. "Identity and the Artistic Process in Yoruba Aesthetic Concept of Ìwà," *Journal of Culture and Ideas* 1 (1) 13-30.

Abiodun, Rowland, H. J. Drewal and J. Pemberton (eds.). 1994. *The Yoruba Artist: New Theoretical Perspectives on African Arts*, Washington and London: Smithsonian Institution Press.

Adeniji, David A. 1975. *Aláṣùwàdà, láti Ẹnú Alàgbà*, Ibadan: Institute of African Studies, University of Ibadan.

Akiwowo, Akinsola. 1983. "Àsùwàdà-Ènìyàn," *Ifè: Annals of the Institute of Cultural Studies* (University of Ifè, Nigeria) 1:113-23.

Akiwowo, Akinsola. 1986. "Contributions to the Sociology of Knowledge from an African Oral Poetry," *International Sociology* 1 (4) 343-58.

Bascom, William R. 1969. *Ifá Divination: Communication between Men and Gods in West Africa*, Bloomington: Indiana University Press.

Bascom. William R. 1980. *Sixteen Cowries: Yoruba Divination from Africa to the New World*, Bloomington: Indiana University Press.

Beyiko, Fagbenro. 1940. *Ifá*, Lagos: The Hope Rising Press.

Beyiko, Fagbenro. 1943. *Ìwé Kíní Agbọ́nniregun*, Lagos: Alafia Press.

Epega, Afolabi A. and Philip John Neimark. 1995. *The Sacred Ifá Oracle*, San Francisco: Harper Collins Publishers.

Epega, D. Onadela. n.d. *Ifá Amònà Áwon Baba Wa*, I-XVI, Ode Remo Omole Oluwa Institute (typewritten) (approimate dates 1948-1957).

Epega, D. Onadela. 1931. *The Mystery of the Yoruba Gods*, Lagos: The Hope Rising Press.

Epega, D. Onadela. 1937. *Ìwé Ifá ati Ìtùmò Àlá*, Lagos: The Hope Rising Press.

Fama, Chief/Ms. 1994. *Sixteen Mythological Stories of Ifá*, San Bernardino: Ilé Òrúnmìlà Communications.

Idowu, E. Bolaji. 1962. *Olódùmarè: God inYoruba Belief*, London: Longman.

Karenga, Maulana. 1984. *Selections from the Husia: Sacred Wisdom of Ancient Egypt*, Los Angeles: University of Sankore Press.

Karenga, Maulana. 1994. *Maat, The Moral Ideal in Ancient Egypt: A Study in Classical African Ethics*, University of Southern California (unpublished dissertation).

Karenga, Maulana. *Kawaida: A Communitarian African Philosophy*, Los Angeles: University of Sankore Press (Publication date: 2000).

Lawal, Babatunde. 1996. *The Gèlèdè Spectacle: Art, Gender, and Social Harmony in an African Culture*, Seattle and London: University of Washington Press.

Lijadu, E. M. 1908. *Òrúnmìlà*!, Hockley: Samuel Richards.

Lijadu, E. M. 1923. *Ifá: Ìmọ̀lẹ̀ Rẹ̀ ti Ìṣe Ìpilẹ̀ Ìsìn ní Ilẹ̀ Yorùbá*, Exeter: James Townsend & Sons.

Popoola, S. Solagbade. 1997. *Practical Ifá, For the Beginner and Professional*, New York: Athelia Henrietta Press.

Sowande, Fela. 1965. *Ifá*, Yaba: Forward Press (c. 1964)

Sowande, Fela. 1965. *Ifá. Odù Mímó*, Lagos: The Ancient Religious Socieites of African Descendents Association. Mimeographed.

Verger, Pierre. 1957. "Grandeur et Décadence du Culte de *Ìyámi Òsòròngá* (Ma Mère la Sorcière) chez la Yoruba," *Journal de la Sociètè des Africanistes* 35 (1) 141-243.

Index